Dictionary of Semiotics

Dictionary of Semiotics

Bronwen Martin
and
Felizitas Ringham

CASSELL
London and New York

Cassell

Wellington House, 125 Strand, London WC2R 0BB

370 Lexington Avenue, New York, NY 10017-6550

First published 2000

British Library Cataloguing-in-Publication Data
A catalogue record for this book is available from the British Library.

ISBN 0-304-70635-3 (hardback)
    0-304-70636-1 (paperback)

Library of Congress Cataloging-in-Publication Data
Martin, Bronwen.
    Dictionary of semiotics / Bronwen Martin and Felizitas
Ringham.
        p. cm.
    Includes bibliographical references and index.
    ISBN 0-304-70635-3. – ISBN 0-304-70636-1 (pbk.)
    1. Semiotics Dictionaries.   I. Ringham, Felizitas.   II. Title.
P99.M357   1999
302.2–dc21   99-20285
                                                                CIP

Sleeping Beauty (pp. 145–7) is reprinted from Tim and Jenny Wood, *Favourite Fairy Tales* (London, 1988) by permission of Conran Octopus.

Typeset by BookEns Ltd., Royston, Herts.
Printed and bound in Great Britain by Biddles Ltd.,
Guildford and King's Lynn

Contents

Preface   vii

How to Use This Dictionary   ix

Introduction   1

Lexical Definitions   15

A Semiotic Analysis of *Sleeping Beauty*   143

Bibliography   168

Index   173

Preface

In the mid-1980s, a professor came to Birkbeck College to give a lecture on semiotics. He was an elderly, relatively short, unassuming gentleman who spoke French and who told us a simple story about a monkey who wanted a banana and needed a stick to get it. The gentleman was the Lithuanian Algirdas Julien Greimas, who introduced us that day – in easy terms – to the semiotic project. Semiotic theory, he informed his audience, is not a branch of philosophy. Rather, it is a practical reflection on discourse, any discourse, not just the verbal sentence. Concerned with values and signification, it tries to unravel the meaning hidden below the surface in an attempt to find sense in life. The monkey and the banana served the purpose to illustrate Greimas's models: keys to understanding how we produce meaning.

This was our first encounter with the founder of the European branch of semiotics. In subsequent years, we were fortunate to meet a number of the Paris semioticians and to attend some of their meetings. Thus we were able to follow at close hand developments of the theory which we have tried to expose in its fundamentals in this small volume. Our enthusiasm for semiotics is shared by more and more people in many different countries. Semiotics is in the air, one might say. It is no longer restricted to literary investigations and academic establishments. Marketing research, the media, law, even visual and gestural discourses make use of the semiotic method. They, like us, believe that semiotics as an analytical tool is shown to be helpful in probing effects of meaning, finding possible answers and even forecasting responses. But more than that: the process of discovery – like that of the explorer in a strange country – opens up the territory of a text, a discourse, to adventures of deeper understanding and new ways of interpretation.

How to Use This Dictionary

Words or expressions/phrases set in italics are in most cases meant to provide cross-references to related entries. The use of bold face is restricted to emphasizing particular words in the context of an entry. Underlining is used to highlight particular words in examples.

How to Use this Dictionary

Introduction

As a literary theory, semiotics has increasingly gained ground in the last two or three decades of the twentieth century. It is now usually included in secondary education literature programmes and in surveys of critical theory. Moreover, the concept has become part of media discourse with regard to film and advertising in Europe and throughout the world. Yet while theoretical research into the discipline has advanced – particularly in France – to many the very term 'semiotics' has remained an enigma and thus its appeal restricted. This book proposes to familiarize researchers as well as university students and their teachers with the semiotic approach. A brief outline of the aims of semiotic theory, its history and working method is followed by a reference section providing definitions of terms and models used in semiotic metalanguage, and finally an example of semiotic analysis applied to a text.

What is semiotics? What does semiotics mean?

The term semiotics is derived from the Greek word *sēmeion* denoting 'sign'. Already in the seventeenth century, the philosopher John Locke referred to *semiotika*, which he defined as '*the Doctrine of Signs*, [...]; the business whereof, is to consider the Nature of Signs, the Mind makes use of for the understanding of Things, or conveying its Knowledge to others'.[1]

In modern usage the concept semiotics refers to a theory of signification. There are different branches of semiotics under this heading. There is an American branch, for instance, strongly influenced by C. S. Peirce, which focuses on logic and meaning and has become central in linguistics linked to philosophy. Much of Peirce's work is devoted to the development of sign categories such as making a distinction between icon, index and symbol.[2] This approach differs considerably from European semiotics, represented by the Paris School (*Ecole de Paris*) founded by A. J. Greimas. The Paris School is concerned primarily with the relationship between signs, and with the manner in which they produce meaning within a given text or discourse.

Importance is attached not only to the elaboration of theories but also to their application as methodological tools for textual analysis. Compared to Peirce, the Paris School thus takes a more wide-reaching approach and, in the final analysis, is of greater practical use. The present dictionary is concerned entirely with the theories and practice of this School.

Semiotics according to the Paris School posits the existence of universal structures that underlie and give rise to meaning. These structures are susceptible to representation in the shape of models which – conversely – can also be applied to any signifying object to decode and interpret its effects of meaning. Being concerned with structures, however, does not mean that semiotics is synonymous with structuralism, a theory concerned solely with the perception and description of structures. Neither is it simply a sign system; it should not be confused with semiology. Nor is it confined to the theories of Roland Barthes. Semiotics, in fact, has a much wider aim: the theory purports to explore the generation of signification, any signification, not only that of the written word, meaning in all its guises and to its full extent. Semiotics thus covers all disciplines and signifying systems as well as social practices and signifying procedures.

Semiotics and the Ecole de Paris: a brief history

In 1985, when speaking about the development of semiotic theory, Greimas said: 'My theoretical genius, if I can so call it, was a form of "bricolage". I took a little Lévi-Strauss and added some Propp ...' He also said that as a linguist, he was more inspired by Dumézil and Lévi-Strauss than by other linguists, 'with the exception of Saussure and Hjelmslev of course'.[3]

It all started at the beginning of the twentieth century with the Swiss linguist Ferdinand de Saussure, who was the first to apply scientific theory to the study of language and to relate this science to social psychology. It was he who introduced the term *sémiologie*, which he defined as forming a link between linguistics and psychology.

Saussure viewed language as a social phenomenon. His great contribution to its study was the discovery that meaning does not reside in individual words but in a complex system of relationships or structures. His motto was: 'Il n'y a de sens que dans la différence.' He pointed out that language structures could be explored by describing them in their current form (synchronically) or historically (diachronically). Saussure is perhaps best known for having divided the phenomenon of language into *langue* (abstract language system, language as structured system of signs) and *parole* (the individual utterances, or speech, making use of the abstract system). In his study of language, however, Saussure went even further. He applied the structure principle to the individual sign or word. The linguistic sign, according to him, is characterized by the relationship of its two components: the 'sound-image' or material substance which he named *signifiant* (signifier) and its 'concept' or *signifié* (signified).

If Saussure and his revolutionary findings[4] paved the way for structuralism and semiotics, the same can be said for the Dane Louis Hjelmslev and the Linguistic Circle of Copenhagen. Even without any immediate link to the Swiss linguist, Hjelmslev's theoretical approach was very close to that of Saussure, whose work he can be said to have continued. In his *Prolegomena to a Theory of Language* (1943) he formalized language, dividing the phenomenon into 'system' and 'process'. Hjelmslev also refined the Saussurian definition of the two aspects of the language-sign by recognizing two fundamental levels or planes of language, one of 'expression' and one of 'content'. Each one of these, he believed, was possessed of a 'substance' and a 'form'. Hjelmslev's contribution to linguistics included his theory of the semiotic function which he defined as existing between the twin aspects of the signifying act – between signifier and signified (according to Saussure) or between expression and content (according to Hjelmslev). Finally, Hjelmslev extended his semiological studies to incorporate non-verbal language systems such as traffic lights or the chimes of Big Ben.

Like Hjelmslev, the anthropologist Claude Lévi-Strauss found a new territory to which he applied a linguistic-structuralist approach. Lévi-Strauss set out to identify the constituent parts of cultural behaviour, which he studied as if it were a language phenomenon. Searching for the semantic structure (the 'language system' or *langue*) that underpins culture, his concern focused on 'myths'. He analysed myths from different cultures and discovered a number of recurrent elements – which he called 'mythemes' (as compared to 'phonemes' or 'morphemes' in linguistics) – and functions that seemed to operate like the components of universal signifying structures.[5]

At the same time an earlier study by the Russian folklorist Vladimir

Propp appeared in English translation.[6] Close analysis of one hundred fairy-tales had led him to establish an analogy between language structure and the organization of narrative. He identified thirty-one functions or fundamental components that formed the basis of any tale. A function in this sense is a unit of the 'narrative language', such as 'a difficult task is proposed to the hero' (25) or 'the villain is punished (30). The thirty-one functions, moreover, were distributed amongst seven spheres of action such as (1) villain, (2) donor, (3) helper, and so on. The narrative taxonomy developed by Propp, as well as his model, is still held to be valid by researchers today.

Such was the groundbase that inspired Greimas to compose the founding work of what was to become semiotics: *Sémantique structurale* (Paris: Larousse, 1966). This seminal text contained the axiomatic base of a scientific theory, anticipated hypotheses for subsequent research and provided samples of semiotic practice, demonstrating its value as a tool for discovery. Nonetheless, this 'ouvrage fondateur' was only the beginning. It marked the starting point of a scientific project which is still today in the process of developing. Over many years, Greimas and a group of researchers dedicated themselves in weekly meetings to elaborating, testing, changing and refining a theory of signification. The meetings took place at the Ecole des Hautes Etudes in Paris, to which Greimas had been appointed. It was there that the Paris School of Semiotics originated.

The development of semiotic theory took place in several phases. The first stage focused, within the context of structuralist thought, on the problematics of semantics as demonstrated by the very title of Greimas's *Sémantique structurale*. Saussure's notion of meaning resulting from relationships had inspired Greimas to analyse and define specific kinds of difference. He first identified the distinctive traits of oppositions in the event producing a typology. Oppositive properties were then categorized to be used as working concepts in the elaboration of a rudimentary signifying structure. At the same time, the encounter with Propp's work encouraged Greimas to apply linguistic models to narrative. In an attempt to formulate better the elements of narrativity, he discovered that what Propp had called 'function' was in fact a verb plus actants, in other words, a complete sentence. He also found that it was possible to reduce Propp's seven spheres of action to three pairs of binary opposition (subject/object; sender/receiver; helper/opponent) that would describe any narrative structure.

4

The theoretical advances made during this first stage of development concerned two apparently heterogeneous areas: on the one hand the search for an elementary structure of meaning comprising the logical classification of paradigmatic differences; and on the other, formulating a theory of narrativity which streamlined Propp's syntagmatic model into the components of a narrative grammar. During the second phase of semiotic research, in the 1970s, attempts were made to find a synthesis between these different fields in order to define a consistent general theory of the generation of meaning.

Concentrating on the surface structures of narrative, semioticians discovered that function, as represented by an action verb, was overdetermined by modalities: two virtualizing (wanting, having to) and two actualizing (knowing how to, being able to). When this discovery was pushed to its extremes, it emerged that the entire narrative grammar was in fact composed merely of modalities plus content, that is, semantics. This allowed for powerful models to be constructed. Moreover, these models could also be applied to social practices, behaviour patterns, etc. Narrativity was no longer seen to be the exclusive property of written texts. From now on it was perceived as underlying all discourse and accounting for the organization of the world.

Research during this period also showed that Propp's formula of the tale could be broken down into important sequences which together reflected the stages of all human action. The sequences – manipulation, action, sanction – were condensed into what came to be known as the canonical narrative schema. This was found to be applicable not only to stories but to a great variety of texts (legal, culinary, journalistic, etc.) and, in the end, to something as basic as man's quest for the meaning of life.

While work on the surface level of narrative structures progressed, essential findings on the abstract or deep level of signification yielded the link needed to perfect semiotic theory. Greimas proposed a visual representation of the elementary structure of meaning: the semiotic square. This is the logical expression of any semantic category showing all possible relationships that define it, i.e. opposition, contradiction and implication. It was discovered, however, that apart from illustrating opposing relationships, this square also portrays the operations they generate. In fact, it allows to retrace a process in progress or the trajectory of a subject performing acts of transformation. In other words: the semiotic square not only represents underlying categories of opposition but also gives account of surface structures of narrative syntax. At the end of the 1970s, all the semiotic findings of the previous two decades were published in an authoritative work by Greimas and Joseph Courtés: *Sémiotique, dictionnaire raisonné de la théorie du langage* (Paris: Hachette, 1979).

The *Dictionnaire* appeared to be evidence of semiotic theory having consolidated: its working concepts were defined seemingly once and for all, its models ready to be applied. This was not so, however. Research continued. The major preoccupation during the years following the publication of the *Dictionnaire* concerned the discursive level of meaning. This level relates to the figurative and enunciative surface of an utterance which gives expression to, and is supported by, the underlying semio-narrative structures. During the 1980s and 1990s, efforts concentrated in particular on aspectualities, that is, the spatial, temporal and actorial organization of texts. Concern with aspectual problematics also lead to renewed investigation of systems of valuation. How does a being, an object, a time or a place assume value? And to whom? The last few semiotic seminars at the Ecole des Hautes Etudes were devoted to the study of 'Truth', 'Beauty', 'Good and Evil' and how these classic values function in language. It was discovered that the system of valuation for each one of them operated along different aspectual lines. Morality, for instance, seemed to fall within the categories of 'excess' and 'insufficiency', while the study of aesthetics revealed the aspects of being accomplished (perfect) or unaccomplished, unfinished (imperfect) as determining factors. This discovery was all the more important as the aspectual categories concerned were not oppositive or binary but gradual. It was not a question of 'either or' but of 'more or less'.

While the new findings added to semiotic knowledge, they also challenged earlier notions including the logical bases of the elementary structure of signification. In 1983, Greimas wrote an article, 'Le Savoir et le Croire: un seul univers cognitif', in which he presented for the first time a semiotic square based on gradual transformation and not on contradiction and oppositive stages.[7] In 1986, the second volume of *Sémiotique, dictionnaire raisonné de la théorie du langage* was published. It reflects both the large numbers of contributors now engaged in research and a science still in the process of being defined.

In his final years Greimas's semiotic concern focused on 'passions' and the thymic sphere. No longer describing passions in terms of modal structures, he and his colleagues now embarked on re-interpreting them in aspectual terms and specific discursive sequences. Simultaneously, attempts were made to define deep-level aspectualties which concern specific valorizations.

Greimas died in 1992. We have only given a very brief outline of his semiotic investigations, and of what in Paris is called basic semiotic theory. The work is by no means completed and research is still in progress. Future findings, however, or even changes if necessary, will not be able to alter the description of the scientific project Greimas set for himself and for us, that is, the study of semiotics, defined as a 'théorie de la signification. Son souci premier sera d'expliciter, sous forme d'une construction conceptuelle, les conditions de la saisie et de la production de sens [...].'[8]

Semiotics as a tool for analysis

What, then, is the semiotic approach? How does it work? Semiotics takes as its fundamental premise that there can be no meaning without difference. There can be no 'up' without 'down', no 'hot' without 'cold', no 'good' without 'evil'. As Greimas says,

> We perceive differences and thanks to that perception, the world 'takes shape' in front of us, and for our purposes.

There are four basic principles on which the semiotic analysis of texts is based:

1. Meaning is not inherent in objects, objects do not signify by themselves. Meaning, rather, is constructed by what is known as a competent observer, i.e. by a subject capable of 'giving form' to objects. To give an example: confronted with an implement from a different culture, say African or Asian, we would probably be incapable of grasping its significance. However, left alone with it, we will give it a meaning that is based on what knowledge we have and what will suit our purpose.

2. Semiotics views the text, any text, as an autonomous unit, that is, one that is internally coherent. Rather than starting with ideas/meanings external to the text and showing how they are reflected within it, an approach that is still widely adopted in the academic

world, semiotic analysis begins with a study of the actual language and structures of the text, showing how meanings are constructed and, of course, at the same time what these meanings are. Semiotic analysis becomes, then, a discovery method and is clearly an invaluable tool for all those engaged in original research.

3. Semiotics posits that story structure or narrativity underlies all discourse, not just what is commonly known as a story. For instance, it underlies political, sociological and legal discourse. One can even go as far as to say that narrativity underlies our very concept of truth: recent studies in the field of legal discourse, for example, have shown that those witnesses in a law court whose account conforms most closely to archetypal story patterns are those whose version is most likely to be believed.

4. Semiotics posits the notion of levels of meaning: it is, for instance, the deep abstract level that generates the surface levels. A text must, therefore, be studied at these different levels of depth and not just at the surface level as is the case with traditional linguistics.

Keeping in mind these principles, semiotic analysis is aided further by *schemas* or *models* whose application contributes to decoding the meaning of texts. We will give a brief survey of the most important of these and explain how they relate to different textual levels.

The discursive level

The discursive level is a surface level of meaning or level of manifestation. Here we examine the specific words – or grammatical items/structures that are visible on the surface of the text. Most grammar teaching – and indeed textual analysis – has hitherto been concerned exclusively with this level. Key elements on this level are:

The *figurative* component: by this we mean all the elements in the text that refer to the external physical world. They are known as figures. Figurative reality, then, is that reality that can be apprehended by the five senses – vision, smell, hearing, taste and touch. It can be contrasted with the inner world of the conceptual abstract, that is the third and deep level of meaning.

To explore the figurative component we start with examining the vocabulary. We try to extract the most important lexical (semantic) fields. This is done by grouping together words that have a meaning in common or a common denominator. These groupings are called 'isotopies' (*isotopies* in French). The lists of isotopies can then be interpreted: How are they distributed in the text? Which is/are the dominant one/s? Can we extract oppositions at this level? This kind of interpretation will already give us an indication of what will be the significant themes.

Grammatical/syntactic features: the use of the active or passive voice, for example, or procedures like nominalization and cohesive markers throw light on the organization of a text and thus reveal textual strategies of manipulation.

The *enunciative* component: this relates to traces of the speaker/author and the listener/reader in the text. What image does the utterance construct of either of them? Investigation of pronouns, of the narrative voice (personalized or depersonalized), of forms of speech (direct/indirect), for instance, indicate signifying intentionality. Most important in this respect is also the modality of a statement, categorical, for example, in the case of news reporting, or tentative on the part of a pupil, etc.

The narrative level

This level is more general and more abstract than the discursive level. It is the level of story grammar or surface narrative syntax, a structure that, according to the Paris School, underpins all discourse, be it scientific, sociological, artistic, etc.

Semiotic analysis of this level of meaning makes use of two fundamental narrative models: (1) the actantial narrative schema and (2) the canonical narrative schema. These models jointly articulate the structure of the quest or, to be more precise, the global narrative programme of the quest. They can be applied to an extract, for example, a single paragraph or to a whole text.

We will first look at the *actantial narrative schema*. This schema presents six key narrative functions (actantial roles) which together account for all possible relationships within a story and indeed within the sphere of human action in general:

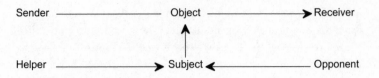

The schema is a simplification of Propp's seven 'spheres of action' or roles elaborated from a study of the Russian folk-tale – such as those of hero, villain, helper, etc. The diagram depicts the following relationships:

1. Subject/object

This is the most fundamental relationship: there can be no subject without an object and vice versa. A subject goes in quest of an object. The object of the quest could be concrete – a person or thing – or abstract, such as knowledge, truth or love.

There is usually more than one subject and more than one quest in, for example, a novel or a newspaper article.

2. Helper/opponent

The subject could be helped or hindered in its quest. Again these actantial positions could be held by objects or internal qualities as well as by people. Money or courage could be my helper and laziness my opponent.

A variant of the opponent is the anti-subject. An anti-subject is a subject who, to achieve its goal, obstructs the quest of another subject. The subject/anti-subject relationship characterizes all fiction and most newspaper articles or TV broadcasts: it is, of course, the hero/villain scenario.

3. Sender/receiver

The sender is an actant (person/idea) that motivates an act or causes something to happen. In other words, the sender provokes action, causes someone to act. The sender transmits to the receiver the desire to act (*vouloir faire*) or the necessity to act (*devoir faire*). We call the desire or obligation to act 'modalities'. What is known as a contract is established between sender and receiver. The receiver, when in possession of one (or both) of the relevant modalities, is transformed into a subject ready to embark on a quest.

We will now look at the *canonical narrative schema*. This presents in detail the different stages of any quest.

Contract/Manipulation	Competence	Performance	Sanction
	Qualifying test	Decisive test	Glorifying test
Persuasive doing	Strengthening	The primary	The subject's
of sender	of desire	event where	performance
Acquisition of a	Acquisition of a	the object of	is recognized
wanting-to-do or	being-able-to-do	value is at	(praise/blame,
having-to-do	and/or knowing-	stake	success/failure)
	how-to-do		

The contract

The sender motivates the action, communicating the modalities of desire or obligation to the receiver. A contract is established, the receiver becomes a subject and embarks on the quest. The contract is followed by three tests:

1. The qualifying test

The subject must acquire the necessary competence to perform the planned action or mission. The desire or obligation to act is in itself not sufficient. The subject must also possess the ability to act (*pouvoir faire*) and/or the knowledge/skills (*savoir faire*) to carry it out. For example, if your intention is to shoot somebody, you first need to acquire a gun. The gun functions as your helper providing you with the necessary ability to act. However, you must also know how to shoot, otherwise the gun is useless. The *being-able-to-do* and the *knowing-how-to-do* are also known as modalities.

2. The decisive test

This represents the principal event or action for which the subject has been preparing, where the object of the quest is at stake. In adventure stories or newspaper articles, the decisive test frequently takes the form of a confrontation or conflict between a subject and an anti-subject.

3. The glorifying test

This is the stage at which the outcome of the event is revealed. The decisive test has either succeeded or failed, the subject is acclaimed or punished. In other words, it is the point at which the performance of the subject is interpreted and evaluated by what is known as the sender-adjudicator. The sender-adjudicator judges whether the performance is in accordance with the original set of values (ideology or mandate) instituted by the initial sender. To distinguish the two senders we call the first one the mandating sender and the second the sender-adjudicator. These roles are not necessarily played by the same actor or person.

When applying these fundamental narrative models to texts, it is important to be aware of several points:

— Each individual text exploits these schemas in its own way. It is highly significant which stages of the quest are explicit, or manifested in the text and which are implicit. The media, for instance, tend to foreground the stage of performance (decisive test) and the stage of sanction (glorifying test).
— Correlations can be made with the discursive level: Figurative elements that have emerged as dominant isotopies or determining oppositions may, on the narrative level, take the positions of object or subject of a quest.
— Not all stories or quests are completed. A quest may be aborted through the successful intervention of an anti-subject: if you set out to sail around the world and your boat capsizes, your quest is rather abruptly terminated.

The deep or abstract level

After analysing the narrative level of meaning, the next stage is to examine the deep level, sometimes also known as the thematic level. This is the level of abstract or conceptual syntax where the fundamental values which generate a text are articulated. These values can be presented in the form of a *semiotic square.*

The semiotic square is a visual presentation of the elementary structure of meaning. Articulating the relationships of contrariety (opposition), contradiction and implication, it is the logical expression of any semantic category.

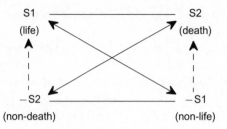

S1 ——————————— S2
(life)   (death)

−S2 ——————————— −S1
(non-death)   (non-life)

(1) S1 and S2 are in a relation of opposition or contrariety (one term presupposes the other).

(2) S1 and −S1 are in a relation of contradiction: −S1 negates S1. S2 and −S2 are also in a relation of contradiction: −S2 negates S2.

(3) −S1 and S2 are in a relation of implication: −S1 implies S2. Similarly, −S2 implies S1.

The semiotic square is a useful tool to illustrate the basic semantic or thematic oppositions underpinning a text. It also makes it possible to show textual dynamics by plotting essential stages or transformations in a story and to follow the narrative trajectory of the subject.

At the end of this book (pp. 148-67) we give an example of a semiotic analysis, in which the approach is applied to a well-known fairy-tale.

Notes

1. John Locke, *An Essay Concerning Human Understanding*, ed. Peter H. Nidditch (Oxford: Clarendon Press, 1975/1979), Book IV, ch. XXI, p. 720.
2. Peirce's ideas have influenced the work of Umberto Eco, who both developed and contested Peirce's categories.
3. Algirdas J. Greimas, 'On meaning', *New Literary History*, 20 (1989), 539-50 (p. 541).
4. They are recorded in Saussure's *Cours de linguistique générale*, which was put together from notes taken by his students of lectures delivered at the University of Geneva between 1906 and 1911, and published posthumously in 1915.
5. See also Claude Lévi-Strauss, *Anthropologie structurale* (Paris: Plon, 1958).

6. Vladimir Propp, *Morphology of the Folktale* (Bloomington: Indiana University Press, 1958).
7. Greimas's article is reproduced in *Du Sens II* (Paris: Seuil, 1983), pp. 115-33.
8. 'the theory of signification. Its first concern shall be to elucidate, through conceptual construction, the conditions for the production and apprehension of meaning [...]', *Dictionnaire* (1979), p. 345.

Lexical Definitions

Absence

The notion absence is defined by the opposite term **presence**. In semiotic terms, absence often denotes existence *in absentia*, that is, virtual existence. For example, the term 'death' implies the absence of life. The concept of life would therefore be present *in absentia* when 'death' is mentioned. Or a text about trains might signify in conjunction with or in opposition to other means of transport which, though not necessarily mentioned, would nonetheless be 'virtually' present in the text.

Abstract

A term is abstract if it refers to a *conceptual*, non-physical universe, i.e. an inner, mental world. An abstract reality is one which cannot be perceived by the five senses: good and evil, love and hate are abstract concepts. Generally accepted abstract values are known as universals.

Abstract notions can be contrasted with the concrete, physical universe: kissing or beating someone with a stick belongs to the concrete world. They are the specific manifestation in time and space of underlying abstract values. The distinction between concrete and abstract, therefore, is expressed in the two levels of meaning: in the figurative (superficial) level of manifestation and on the deep level. Crying, for example, could be an indication of sorrow, or killing one of evil.

See also *concrete* and *conceptual*.

Achrony

The term achrony affirms the atemporal nature of logico-semantic structures. Semiotic structures on a deep level are achronic whereas discursive structures (e.g. those of the figurative level) exist 'in time' and call for temporalization. In Robert Louis Stevenson's story of *Treasure Island*, for example, events are arranged and signify in temporal sequence. Moreover, the hero, Jim Hawkins, sets a temporal framework for the story from its very beginning by telling us that he is old yet writing about himself as a young boy. The deep-level structures of the tale, on the other hand, involving social and moral order and disorder, being and not-being, are achronic, their logical relationships and dynamics not being subject to time.

See also *diachrony* and *synchrony*.

Acquisition

Acquisition belongs to the discursive level of discourse. Paradigmatically opposed to deprivation or lack, the term designates the act or transformation that brings about the conjunction of a subject and an object of value. Acquisition can be brought about in two ways:

1. in a transitive manner through a process of **attribution**: the subject acquires an object of value through the action of another object. For example, your mother may give you £5000.

2. In a reflexive manner through a process of **appropriation**: the subject acquires the object of value through its own action. For example, you may go exploring to find the hidden treasure.

In terms of the actantial narrative schema, acquisition represents the successful outcome of a quest.

See also *lack*.

Actant

An actant is someone or something who or which accomplishes or undergoes an act. It may be a person, anthropomorphic or zoomorphic agent, a thing or an abstract entity.

Situated on the level of narrative syntax, the term describes a narrative function such as that of subject or object. In the sentence 'Prison officers vote for work to rule which could bring jails to a standstill', 'work to rule' in the first part of the sentence functions as actant/object of the prison officers' quest while 'which' (referring to the same 'work to rule') in the second part of the sentence functions as actant/subject capable of bringing about a transformation. In the fairy-tale *Sleeping Beauty*, the prince functions as actant/subject in his own quest to marry the beautiful princess and as actant/helper in the quest to break the spell of the nasty fairy godmother.

Actant has to be distinguished from actor, a term used when describing the discursive organization.

See also *actor*.

Actantial narrative schema

This is a fundamental universal narrative structure that underlies all texts. There are six key actantial roles or functions arranged in three sets of binary opposition: subject/object; sender/receiver; helper/opponent. Together the six actants and their organization account for all possible relationships within a story and indeed within the sphere of human action in general:

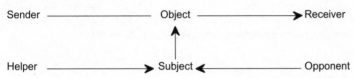

The role of anti-subject, a variant of the opponent, may also be included within this diagram. These narrative positions may be held by people, places, objects or abstract ideas.

The diagram illustrates in the first place the necessary relationship between a sender and a receiver. This is based on the desire for an object or on an obligation which the sender transmits to the receiver, inducing the latter to pursue it. The function of the sender therefore is to make the receiver do something (*faire faire*), thereby turning the receiver into a subject.

The relationship between the subject and the object, on the other hand, also based on desire or obligation, is geared to change a state of being (*faire être*): its function is to transform a state of deficiency or wanting into one of sufficiency through conjunction with or disjunction from an object. Helper and opponent entertain a subsidiary relationship to the subject, their function being to intervene positively or negatively in the pursuit of the goal. Thus the desire for an object becomes the focal point of the whole scheme. Examples illustrating the different functions are to be found under separate headings for each particular actant.

Action

In semiotics, the term action designates a series of acts or transformations organized in a logical sequence (narrative trajectory). Accordingly, an action is a narrative programme in which an actor is engaged in concrete acts at a specific time and in a specific place. In other words, action describes the stages of competence and performance of the canonical narrative schema. The action in *Treasure Island* consists of the voyage to the island (stage of competence) and the search for the treasure (stage of performance).

The analysis of narrated actions enables us to recognize stereotypes of human activities and to construct typological and syntagmatic models which take account of them. These models form the basis of a semiotics of action.

See also *canonical narrative schema* and *narrative trajectory*.

Actor

Semiotics uses the term actor to refer to any individual, anthropo-morphic or zoomorphic agent, to a group (e.g. a crowd) or to an abstract entity such as fate that is perceptible on the *discursive* level of an utterance and plays a part in a story. In semiotic analysis, actor has replaced the traditional terms of 'character' or 'protagonist'. Actors are individualized and represent concrete figurative elements. In the fairy-tale *Cinderella*, the main actors are Cinderella herself, her sisters, the fairy godmother and the prince.

The term should be distinguished from **actant**, which is more abstract and refers to a narrative function.

See also *actant*.

Actorialization

The term actorialization refers to the process whereby actors are established in discourse. Like spatialization and temporalization, it is a necessary ingredient in the production of a referential illusion or reality effect. To be an actor you must possess at least one thematic role (a socially defined 'theme' or function) and one narrative function (such as subject or object of a quest). Example: A poor fisherman (thematic role) wants to marry (designating the fisherman as subject of a quest) the beautiful princess (thematic role plus object of the quest).

See also *spatialization, temporalization* and *thematic role*.

The term actualization designates one of two basic modes of semiotic existence: virtual and actual. Actualizing modalities are knowing (*savoir*) and being able to do or to be (*pouvoir*). With regard to language, actualization denotes the operation by which any given language unit is rendered 'present' within a particular linguistic context. Resulting actual existence (*in praesentia*) characterizes the syntagmatic axis of language, that is, the sentence in the speech flow (*parole*) as opposed to the language system (*langue*) from which individual units are selected. Any lexeme, for example, has only virtual existence until it becomes actualized in the context that turns it into a sememe.

Narrative semiotics replaces the couple virtualization/actualization with the ternary virtualization/actualization/realization in order to describe accurately all possible kinds of junction between a subject and an object. Before any junction has been specified, subjects and objects are in *virtual* positions. Their position is *realized* once subject and object are conjoined. When, however, they are in a state of disjunction, they are termed *actualized*. This kind of actualization relates to two possible moments in a quest:

1. It applies when the subject of a quest has acquired competence but has not yet reached the stage of performance and is therefore still disjoined from its object of value. Example: When Bluebeard's wife has obtained the key to the rooms she is not allowed to open, her quest can be described as actualized. Once she has transgressed the taboo, opened the door and seen the horrible truth, she is conjoined with the object of value (knowledge) and the positions are thus realized.

2. Actualization also relates to a state of disjunction that succeeds a quest which has been realized. Example: When Cinderella wishes for a dress to go to the ball, the dress has only virtual existence (*in absentia*) for her. Once her fairy godmother has produced the garment and given it to Cinderella, subject and object are conjoined and are therefore realized. After the ball, the garment has been returned, subject and object are again disjoined and in the event are merely actualized. In other words, actualization here corresponds with a transformation which amounts to an operation

of disjunction. This, on the discursive level, is often tantamount to deprivation.

See also *lexeme, realization, sememe* and *virtualization.*

Adjudicator

The term adjudicator denotes the actor who judges the success or failure of a subject's performance in a quest. A teacher takes the role of an adjudicator when s/he judges a pupil's performance by giving him/ her a good (or bad) mark. The little boy judges his own action when saying 'I did a brave thing'. In this case we talk of auto-adjudication.

Judging a subject's performance is the last stage in the structure of a narrative. It is called the glorifying test or sanction. The judge here is normally called sender-adjudicator since this instance often, though not always, also functions in establishing the initial contract with the subject pursuing a quest.

See also *canonical narrative schema* and *sender-adjudicator.*

Aesthetics

The term aesthetics designates the theory of the experience of beauty or the philosophy of taste and art. Normally, aesthetic perception is a mixture of appreciation and pleasure which we experience, for instance, when listening to music, admiring a painting or being faced with a spectacular sunset.

The semiotician A. J. Greimas attaches aesthetics to the notion of perfection. He believes the aesthetic experience to reside in a momentary glimpse of a wholeness of life which goes beyond rational explanation. Semiotically, the event could be described as subject and object, for a brief instant, blending into one. The positive joy produced by this event links it to the thymic category. An example of such an aesthetic experience in literature would be Proust's tasting of the *madeleine* which gave rise to his famous work *A la recherche du temps perdu.*

See also *thymic.*

Semiotics employs the term agent (or operating agent) to designate the narrative role of a **subject of doing**, that is, of a subject engaged in the carrying out of a particular narrative programme. It contrasts with the term **patient** which designates a **subject of state**. In the sentence 'The knight slays the dragon', the knight is the operating agent. Equally, in the sentence 'The electorate opted for Labour', the body of electors is the agent carrying out its role in the narrative programme of the poll.

See also *patient, subject of doing* and *subject of state*.

Alethic modalities (*modalités aléthiques*)

In semiotic theory the modal structure known as alethic is produced when an utterance of state is governed by a modal utterance of obligation or possibility (having-to-be; being possible/impossible). For instance: 'She had to be very clever', 'They did not have to be in London for the event', 'It was impossible to be generous', 'It was possible to make the journey within the time given'.

The alethic modal structure can be projected onto the semiotic square as follows:

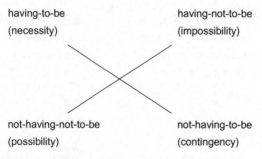

having-to-be	having-not-to-be
(necessity)	(impossibility)
not-having-not-to-be	not-having-to-be
(possibility)	(contingency)

See also *having-to-do* and *modalities*.

Anachronism

An anachronism is the setting of an event, scene, person or object in the wrong historical period. The most famous example is the clock in Shakespeare's *Julius Caesar*.

Analysis

The term analysis designates procedures employed to describe a semiotic object. Considering any semiotic object as a signifying whole, these procedures aim to establish, on the one hand, relationships among the different components of the object and on the other, between its constituents and the whole.

Procedures, moreover, focus on different aspects. *Syntactic analyses* concentrate on narrative grammar. They investigate narrative functions and actorial roles such as those of the wolf and the grandmother in *Little Red Riding Hood* and how they relate to each other. *Semic analyses*, by contrast, compare units of meaning. What do units of meaning such as mother/child/wolf/grandmother have (or have not) in common? Are they related? What separates them?

See also *function, seme, sememe* and *syntax.*

Anaphora

An anaphora serves to link two utterances, two paragraphs, etc. by using a connecting term referring back to some concept already mentioned. In the example 'John came into the room. He was wearing a new coat', the pronoun 'he' functions as an anaphora.

Anaphorization is one of the main procedures that enable the enunciator (addresser) to establish and maintain interphrastic textual continuity/cohesion. It is one of the methods whereby internal networks of meaning are set up.

See also *cataphora.*

Anthropomorphic

The term anthropomorphic refers to the representation of animals or lifeless things as though endowed with human attributes such as feelings or speech.

'The mountain spewed its breath of death and exhaled its milky vapours' (Guy de Maupassant, *Two Friends*).

Anthroponym

An anthroponym is the designation of actors by their proper names such as 'Joanne' or 'Paul'. Like toponyms, they contribute to the creation of an illusion or simulacrum of the real. They are, therefore, a key component of the process of figurativization.

See also *chrononym, simulacrum* and *toponym.*

Antiphrasis

The term antiphrasis describes a figure of speech whereby one word in a sentence is used in a sense directly opposite to its literal or usual meaning. As a result, an effect of irony is produced. Drenched by rain and shivering with cold, one might, for example, talk of the 'beautiful sunny' weather or refer to an exceptionally ugly person as 'Mr Handsome'.

Anti-sender

The anti-sender represents an actantial instance (person or idea) in conflict with the principal sender and its programme. As a result the anti-sender not only institutes a system of values that opposes the original quest but also attempts to manipulate the receiver/subject to act in a way contrary to the desires of the first sender. In the case of a strike, the sender of the employees' quest may be a trade union leader (as well as a sense of social justice) whose aim is to persuade them to stop work. The anti-sender here is the employer whose goal is to persuade the employees (by means of threats etc.) to continue work or return to it.

See also *sender.*

Anti-subject

A story may contain two or more subjects whose quests are in conflict. An anti-subject is a subject who, to achieve its goal, obstructs the quest of another subject. The wolf in *Little Red Riding Hood* is the anti-subject who obstructs the little girl's quest to see her grandmother in order to pursue his own goal of eating her. In the fight for a territory two opposing armies may each take up the positions of subject or anti-subject, depending on the point of view from which events are reported.

See also *opponent.*

Antonym

The term antonym designates a particular type of oppositeness. 'Boy' and 'girl' are antonyms because they oppose each other while sharing a semantic feature, that is, they possess the common denominator: children. Similarly, the antonyms 'hot' and 'cold' possess temperature in common, 'high' and 'low' verticality, etc.

When pairs of opposites occur in proximity to each other in a text, they exert a marked cohesive effect. To give an example: 'At least 125 people died of AIDS in Bulawayo between April and June this year, according to City Health authorities … Out of the 125, 71 were males while 54 were females.'

In semiotic theory the word antonym can be replaced by the term seme. The semes 'high' and 'low', for example, articulate the semantic category of verticality.

See also *lexical cohesion, semantic category* and *synonym.*

Aphoria

Aphoria is the neutral term of the thymic category euphoria versus dysphoria. Examples: 'The death of the cat did not make her feel particularly happy or sad'; 'He was indifferent to the loss of his money'.

See also *thymic.*

Appropriation

The term appropriation designates the transformation whereby a subject of state acquires an object of value through its own efforts, i.e. through a reflexive act. For example, I (subject of state) buy (doing of which 'I' am the subject) two tickets for the play (object of value). In abstract terms, this is represented in the following way:

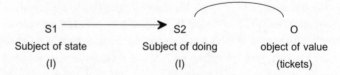

S1	→	S2		O
Subject of state		Subject of doing		object of value
(I)		(I)		(tickets)

Appropriation can be contrasted with attribution where the subject of state acquires an object of value thanks to a subject of doing other than itself, i.e. it represents a transitive act. For example, my mother gives me some apples.

See also *attribution, subject of doing* and *subject of state*.

Aspectualization

The term aspectualization refers to the process whereby the implied presence of an observer is established in the discourse. It involves the spatial, temporal and actorial co-ordinates set up by the utterance which characterize and position the observation. In spatial terms, for example, reference to objects placed on the left or on the right is only meaningful in relation to an implied point of observation. Temporal aspectualization makes itself felt in the stopping and starting of enunciative (or discursive) events; or in the duration of a process on the syntagmatic axis or the punctuality (lack of duration) of a process on the paradigmatic axis of the discourse. In *Treasure Island* the evocation of the length of the sea voyage as well as its punctuation by significant events are founded on aspectual techniques in the novel.

The procedures involved in aspectualization are closely linked to those of *débrayage*.

See also *débrayage*.

Attribution

Attribution designates the transformation whereby a subject of state acquires an object of value thanks to a subject of doing other than itself, i.e. attribution represents a transitive act. I may, for example, acquire wealth – my object of value – when my rich uncle gives me a million pounds. In abstract terms, this is represented in the following way:

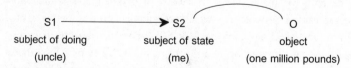

S1	S2	O
subject of doing	subject of state	object
(uncle)	(me)	(one million pounds)

Attribution can be contrasted with appropriation, where the subject of state and the subject of doing are represented by the same actor, i.e. the act is reflexive. For example, I go out and buy a loaf of bread.

See also *appropriation, subject of doing* and *subject of state*.

Author

The term author describes the sender of a message or discourse. We speak of the author of a written text or of any sign system that emanates from a competent source intent on transmitting a message.

In semiotics, the term enunciator is used in preference to author.

See also *enunciator/enunciatee* and *reader*.

Axiology

In general terms, axiology relates to the theory and/or description of systems of value. In a semiotic perspective, the term axiology is used for value systems arranged on a *paradigmatic* axis. In other words, values in axiological structures, while occupying the same place within a narrative syntax, signify in systems of equivalence or opposition. For example, good or honesty (equivalent values) oppose evil (contrasting value); the thymic term euphoria is in opposition to dysphoria.

The term **ideology** is reserved for the *syntagmatic* arrangement of values, that is, their organization in an actantial perspective. Subjects (individual or collective) express or desire values which become objects of a quest. The values themselves are part of axiological systems which, for example, place 'virtue' opposite 'vice'; their selection and actual pursuit in particular instances, on the other hand, define an ideology. The stories of the Bible are an example of values arranged and displayed to form an ideology, in this case that of the Christian faith.

See also *ideology*.

Axiomatic

The term axiomatic relates to a body of non-definable and/or non-demonstrable propositions which are interdefined and demonstrated by means of an arbitrary decision. An axiomatic concept, therefore, permits the construction of a theory by deductive steps. This process contrasts with traditional scientific practice which proceeds from a set of hypotheses and aims at proving them with the data of experience.

Being

The term being possesses at least two meanings:

1. It serves as a copula (link word) in utterances of state. Example: 'Mary was ill'. Such utterances characterize descriptive passages. Together with utterances of doing they make up a narrative.

   In semiotic terms, being expresses a relation of conjunction or disjunction between a subject of state and an object. Examples: 'The sky is blue'; here 'the sky' (subject of state) is in conjunction with the object of value, i.e. blueness. In the utterance 'The man is not rich', on the other hand, the subject of state, 'man', is in disjunction with the object, 'wealth'.

2. The term being is also used to name the modal category of veridiction: being/seeming. This modal category is often brought into play in stories relating to acts of treachery or deception where the hero/heroine is not what s/he appears to be. In the story of *Aladdin*, for example, the exchange of Aladdin's old lamp for a new one appears to his wife to be an act of generosity (seeming) whereas we (the reader) know that it is theft and that the old lady is a villain in disguise (being).

   The opposition being versus seeming can also be paralleled with the dichotomy immanence versus manifestation. Being here relates to the plane of underlying structure (immanence) whereas seeming relates to the plane of outward manifestation.

See also *veridiction*.

Being-able

The modal structure of being-able governs utterances both of doing and of state.

1. Utterances of doing: being-able-to-do. Examples: 'He was unable to contain his anger'; 'You can refuse to come; there is nothing to stop you'; 'We could not decipher your handwriting'; 'The children were unable to swim in the lake'; 'I shall certainly be able to come to the party'.

   This modal structure can be mapped onto the following semiotic square:

Being-able

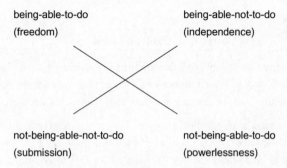

being-able-to-do
(freedom)

being-able-not-to-do
(independence)

not-being-able-not-to-do
(submission)

not-being-able-to-do
(powerlessness)

In the canonical narrative schema the acquisition of a being-able-to-do is a key component of the stage of competence: without possessing this modality of being-able-to-do, the subject cannot proceed to the next stage of the quest, that is, the decisive test or performance.

2. Utterances of state: being-able-to-be. Examples: 'He was sure that one day he could be happy'; 'The money could not have been there'; 'I might be wrong but I don't think so'; 'He must be poor'.

This modal structure can be mapped onto the following semiotic square:

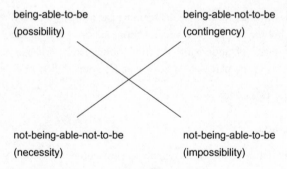

being-able-to-be
(possibility)

being-able-not-to-be
(contingency)

not-being-able-not-to-be
(necessity)

not-being-able-to-be
(impossibility)

See also *canonical narrative schema* and *modalization*.

Believing-to-be

Believing-to-be is a synonym (i.e. the syntactic definition) of the notion of *certainty*. It constitutes the positive term of the epistemic modal category and can be mapped onto the semiotic square as follows:

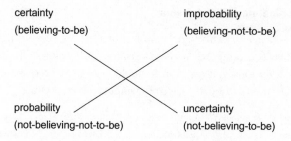

certainty
(believing-to-be)

improbability
(believing-not-to-be)

probability
(not-believing-not-to-be)

uncertainty
(not-believing-to-be)

Example: Frank believes to be in love with Tina = he is <u>certain</u> he is in love. Tina, on the other hand, thinks that she is <u>probably</u> in love with Frank = she does not believe that she is not in love, while Max believes not to be in love = his feelings are at the opposite end of Frank's. The different (or changing) positions of certainty and uncertainty of the actors can thus be plotted on the semiotic square.

See also *uncertainty*.

Binarism

Binarism is an epistemological concept which holds that the structure of binary opposition is one of the characteristics of the human mind. The concept owes much to the work of Roman Jakobson.

Binary

A binary structure refers to a relationship between two terms that are mutually exclusive: up versus down; hot versus cold; good versus evil; etc.

There are two types of binary opposition: (a) that of **contradiction**: cold versus not cold; and (b) that of **contrariety**: cold versus hot. These two types of opposition were developed by Greimas in his formulation of the semiotic square which outlines the elementary structure of meaning.

See also *semiotic square*.

Canonical narrative schema

This schema presents a universal prototype for the structure of narrative. It is composed of three tests: the qualifying test, the decisive test and the glorifying test, which unfold in a logical succession. These tests are preceded by the stage of manipulation or contract.

Contract/Manipulation	Competence	Performance	Sanction
	Qualifying test	Decisive test	Glorifying test
Persuasive doing	Strengthening	The primary	The subject's
of sender	of desire	event where	performance
Acquisition of a	Acquisition of	the object of	is recognized
wanting-to-do or a	a being-able-	value is at	(praise/blame,
having-to-do	to-do and/or	stake	success/failure)
	knowing-how-		
	to-do		

This narrative macro-structure can be exploited by individual texts in a variety of different ways. Certain stages or tests may be foregrounded, others remain implicit: in adventure stories, for example, the emphasis is on the decisive test, whereas legal discourse is centred more on the stage of sanction.

Contract/manipulation: The sender transmits to the receiver the desire or obligation to act. What is known as a contract is established between the two and the subject embarks on a quest. The contract is followed by three tests. These tests mirror the fundamental logic of human action:

The qualifying test (or stage of competence): Here the subject acquires the necessary competence needed to carry out the planned action or mission. The desire or obligation to act is not in itself sufficient: the subject must also possess the ability to act (*pouvoir faire*) and/or the knowledge/skills to do so (*savoir faire*). For example, if your intention is to shoot someone, you first of all need to acquire a gun; the gun functions as your helper, providing you with the necessary ability to act.

The decisive test (or stage of performance): This represents the principal event or action for which the subject has been preparing, where the object of the quest is at stake. In adventure stories or newspaper articles, the decisive test frequently takes the form of a confrontation or conflict between a subject and an anti-subject.

The glorifying test (or sanction): The outcome of the event is now revealed, the decisive test has either succeeded or failed, the subject is acclaimed or punished. In other words, it is the point at which the performance of the subject is interpreted and evaluated by what is known as the sender-adjudicator.

For more details see under individual headings.

Cataphora

Like an anaphora, a cataphora serves to produce textual continuity or cohesion through a network of internal references. Unlike the anaphora, however, a cataphora marks a referral back that precedes mention of the term to which it refers. Put more simply, a cataphora refers forward whereas an anaphora refers back. In the sentence 'It was wonderful, that wedding', 'it' exemplifies a cataphora.

See also *anaphora.*

Category

See *semantic category.*

Certainty

The term certainty designates the positive pole of the epistemic modal category. Its syntactic definition is believing-to-be.

See also *believing-to-be, epistemic modalities* and *uncertainty.*

Chrononym

The term chrononym designates a specific length of time such as 'day', 'spring' or 'coffee break'. Together with anthroponyms and toponyms, chrononyms help to create the referential illusion and are associated, therefore, with the figurative level of meaning.

See also *anthroponym* and *toponym.*

Classeme

A classeme is a generic seme such as human, animal, inanimate, concrete. In other words, it refers to a particular class of objects. Dog, cat, hamster and mouse all belong to the generic class of house animals.

See also *seme*.

Code

The term code designates one of the six elements that make up Jakobson's model of communication. In order to function properly, that is, in order for it to be effectively transmitted, a message must contain a code that is understood by both sender (addresser) and receiver (addressee). In other words, there must be some measure of agreement about the meanings of the words used (or of the gestures, movements, colours, sounds).

Shared assumptions on the figurative level, to offer an example, might be the use of the term 'night' to indicate darkness, or a time to sleep. On the symbolic level, on the other hand, 'light' and 'height' are commonly associated with 'spirituality', 'goodness' or 'truth' whereas 'darkness' and 'depth' might suggest 'error' and 'evil'. Likewise, the term 'Jupiter' evokes a Roman god, and so on.

It must be noted that some cultural codes vary according to their place of origin. A reference to 'Jupiter', for instance, might be incomprehensible to Chinese peasants.

See also *communication model*.

Cognitive

There are two fundamental dimensions of narrative, the pragmatic and the cognitive. The *pragmatic* dimension relates to external physical events such as killing a giant, or catching a thief. The cognitive dimension, on the other hand, relates to internal mental activities such as knowing, convincing, deceiving. The importance attached to each dimension varies according to the nature of the discourse. In adventure stories, for example, it is the pragmatic dimension that dominates, whereas in legal discourse, it is the cognitive.

In recent years attention has been focused on a third dimension of narrative known as the *thymic* dimension. This relates to the feelings of euphoria and dysphoria (i.e. pleasant or unpleasant) experienced by the actors. These feelings can be correlated with the stages of a narrative programme. They can, for example, describe a state of disjunction or conjunction with the object of value. In Flaubert's *Madame Bovary*, Emma's disjunction with money and status gives rise to feelings of dysphoria expressed in terms of grief and frustration.

See also *pragmatic* and *thymic*.

Coherence

In discourse analysis the term coherence designates the extent to which a discourse is perceived to 'hang together' rather than being a set of unrelated sentences or utterances. The linguist Michael Halliday distinguishes between the notions of cohesion and coherence. Whereas cohesion relates to the formal (i.e. *explicit*) links between parts of a text, coherence relates to all those links that are *implicit*, such as reference to cultural and historical context or reference to underlying models or schemata.

The implicit plays a key role in the construction of meaning: a text that relies solely on surface linguistic linking would not make sense.

See also *cohesion* and *connector*.

Cohesion

Cohesion describes the process whereby sentences or utterances are linked together to form a text. Cohesive devices (or ties) are those words or phrases which enable the writer/speaker to establish relationships across sentence or utterance boundaries and which help to link the different parts of the text together. Continuity of meaning is thus achieved.

There are four ways in which cohesion is created. Three of these are grammatical: reference, ellipsis and conjunction; the fourth is lexical. Common cohesive devices are the use of pronouns (functioning as anaphora), repetition, synonyms and collocation.

To give an example:

(a): Have you seen the <u>books</u>? (b): No, I don't know where <u>they</u> are.

The pronoun 'they' refers back to 'books', thus establishing a cohesive tie between the two sentences.

Specialists in discourse analysis make a distinction between the concepts of cohesion and coherence. Whereas cohesion refers to explicit cohesive devices within a text, coherence relates to background knowledge and context. It includes, for example, all those implicit assumptions or presuppositions without which a text would not make sense.

See also *conjunction, ellipsis, lexical cohesion* and *reference*.

Collective

A collective actant is a collection of individuals endowed with a particular narrative role. In accounts of a strike, the strikers could represent a collective actant. They could be the *subject* of a quest (to change working conditions) which is in conflict with an *anti-subject*, also played by a collective actant, the management whose goal it is to maintain the status quo and ensure that work is continued.

The term collective can also be used to describe a semantic universe based on the opposition nature versus culture. An example would be the semantic universe of a traditional American Western.

See also *individual*.

Collocation

Used in linguistics, the term collocation refers to a grouping of all those items in a text that are semantically related. The following items are examples of lexical collocation because they belong to the scientific field of biology: plants, synthesia, organic, sunlight. We can also say that the above terms make up the lexical field of biology.

The term collocation was coined by M. Halliday and is now extensively used in discourse analysis.

See also *lexical field*.

Communication model

For the linguist Roman Jakobson all communication involves six

elements or functions which together make up any speech event
(speech act). The following diagram, devised by Jakobson, illustrates
these elements and their relations:

CONTEXT

ADDRESSER | MESSAGE | ADDRESSEE
(Sender) | CONTACT | (Receiver)
| CODE |

Communication, then, consists of a *message*, initiated by an addresser
(sender) whose destination is an addressee (receiver). The message
requires a *contact* between addresser and addressee which may be oral,
visual, etc. This contact must be formulated in terms of a shared *code* –
speech, numbers, writing, etc. – that makes the message intelligible.
Lastly, the message must refer to a *context* understood by both
addresser and addressee which enables the message to make sense.
Any one of these elements may dominate in a particular communicative
act.

Jakobson's central point is that the 'message' cannot supply all of the
meaning of a transaction. 'Meaning' derives also from the context, the
code and the means of contact, in other words, meaning resides in the
total act of communication.

For more details see under individual headings.

Comparative reference

Comparative reference is a means by which cohesion is strengthened in
a text. A relationship of contrast is being set up with one entity being
compared to another. It may, for example, be the same or different,
equal or unequal, more or less etc. Any expression such as the same,
another, similar, different, as big as, bigger, less big, and related adverbs
such as likewise, differently, equally, presumes some point of reference
in the preceding text. Examples: 'John has a beautiful, expensive car.
Paul's car is different, less expensive but more practical. Peter has the
same car but an older model.'

Comparative reference items can also be used cataphorically (to point
forward). In the phrase 'much more beautiful than her picture', for

37

instance, the reference point for 'more beautiful' lies in what follows. The same applies to the sentence 'John has a bigger apple than Lizzy'.

Competence

By competence is meant the possession of those qualities that make it possible to carry out an action. These qualities are known as the modalities. A subject needs first:

(a) a wanting-to-do (*vouloir faire*) and/or (b) a having-to-do (*devoir faire*).

All action presupposes the desire and/or the necessity to act. The decision to look for buried treasure on a desert island, for example, must be motivated by a particular desire or need: it could be economic deprivation that impels me to embark on the quest – as indeed is the case in many fairy-tales.

A subject in possession only of the desire and/or need to act is known as a *virtual* subject. To become an actualized subject and to become fully competent, the subject must in addition possess the capability to act. It must therefore possess at least one of the following modalities:

(a) a being-able-to-do (*pouvoir faire*) and/or (b) a knowing-how-to-do (*savoir faire*).

Thus, doing itself presupposes a wanting-to-do (or having-to-do) as well as a being-able-to-do (and/or knowing-how-to-do). In my quest for the buried treasure, for example, I will need to acquire a ship or other means of transport. Maps and tools such as a shovel could also be my helpers providing me with the necessary competence.

The four modalities can be considered as objects with which the subject must be conjoined in order to carry out the performance. Modal objects – which constitute competence – can thus be distinguished from the object of value (which is at stake in the performance). The abstract representation of the competent subject is as follows:

S⌒Om

The qualifying test is the series of narrative programmes in which the subject acquires or manifests competence.

See also *modalities* and *qualifying test*.

Complementary

A complementary term is a term that is implied by another within the same semantic category. In the semantic category of 'existence', for example, 'death' and 'non-life' are complementary terms, as are those of 'non-death' and 'life'.

See also *semantic category* and *semiotic square.*

Conative function

When a communication is angled towards the addressee or receiver of the message, drawing him/her into the exchange, then it is the conative function that dominates. This function is indicated by the use of direct questions, warnings or persuasive devices. Questionnaires gathering information about their addressees are an example of texts whose predominant function is conative. The primary function of a party political broadcast may be conative in that it is trying to persuade the listener/viewer to adopt a particular set of opinions and vote for a particular party.

Dominance of the conative function in a text does not preclude the other speech functions being present to varying degrees.

See also *communication model.*

Conceptual

The term conceptual refers to the sphere or inner mental world of abstract ideas. In semiotics the term thematic is frequently employed in the place of conceptual to denote the world of abstract concepts such as those of good and evil, totalitarianism and democracy, freedom and imprisonment, etc.

The conceptual can be contrasted with the figurative, that is, with those elements representing the physical and concrete world that can be apprehended through the five senses.

See also *figurative.*

Concrete

A term is concrete if it possesses a referent in the external physical world, i.e. if it refers to a reality that can be perceived by the five senses.

Concrete

Concrete terms make up what is known as the figurative level of meaning. They are contrasted with abstract, conceptual terms to be found on the deep level.

Concrete terms can have a wealth of meanings depending on the context in which they are used, in other words they have a high semic density. Abstract terms, on the other hand, are much simpler and have low semic density. The term 'car', for instance, in addition to the concrete object may also signify 'speed', 'freedom' or 'prestige' etc., whereas the abstract concepts 'freedom' or 'prestige' are restricted in their meanings.

See also *abstract* and *semic density*.

Configuration

Semiotic theory distinguishes between discursive configurations and lexical configurations. *Discursive* configurations centre on particular expressions or discursive figures revealing underlying immutable structures. The term 'strike', for instance, implies a polemical confrontation staging opposing subjects who are motivated by a sender and an anti-sender. Manipulation, persuasive and interpretative doing are involved, leading to quests failing or being accomplished. Thus the configuration accompanying 'strike' presents itself as a micro-narrative programme (PN *d'usage*) which is to be integrated into larger discursive units within which it acquires functional significance. In this sense, the term configuration in semiotics signifies in a similar way to that of the nineteenth-century concept *motif*.

On a *lexical* level, the term configuration designates the relationships different semantic fields (isotopies) entertain with each other within a particular textual space. For example, a text may be about 'birth' and 'death', about 'work', 'subsistence', 'feelings' and 'time'. All these isotopies would therefore be found independently on the figurative level. In conjunction, however, they can be viewed and evaluated in a configurative perspective.

See also *motif* and *narrative programme*.

Confrontation

The term confrontation describes the polemical structure underpinning narrative programmes in opposition. There are always at least two subjects pursuing quests that are in conflict. The outcome of confrontation, however, varies: either it results in the domination of one or the other of the subjects and their quests, or it leads to an exchange or, more generally, a contract.

To offer a few examples: industrial strikes or wars between nations frequently illustrate confrontation culminating in the domination of one or the other side. Employers achieving a return to work without granting an increase in salary, for instance, is a case in point. On the other hand, negotiations, agreement or a peace treaty, can also be – and sometimes are – the consequence of confrontation in personal quarrels or even between warring nations.

Conjunction

Conjunction is a cohesive device for marking logical relationships in discourse. According to the linguists Michael Halliday and Ruqaiya Hasan (1976) there are four types of logical relationship: additive (designated by conjunctions such as 'and'); adversative (indicated by words such as 'but', 'nevertheless', 'however'); causal (e.g. 'because', 'for'); and temporal (e.g. 'firstly', 'then', 'next', 'while').

Example: 'Very few people are eating beef at present. This is because they are afraid of catching mad-cow disease.' 'Because' here is a causal conjunction.

In discourse analysis, the term conjunction is frequently replaced by the word 'connective' or 'connector'.

See also *cohesion* and *connector*.

Conjunction and disjunction

In semiotic theory, the terms conjunction and disjunction articulate two possible relationships between a subject and an object. In the utterance 'Cinderella is happy', the subject, Cinderella, is in a relationship of conjunction with the object, happiness. In the utterance 'Cinderella is not happy', the relationship between Cinderella and her object, happiness, is one of disjunction.

A narrative programme can be described as the transformation of a syntactical relationship between a subject and an object from one of conjunction to one of disjunction, or vice versa.

See also *narrative programme*.

Connector

A connector is a link word (or a group of words) that binds the parts of a text together thus signalling (i.e. rendering explicit) a logical relationship. It constitutes a key device, therefore, in the creation of textual cohesion.

Connectors may take the form of individual words ('then', 'but'), set phrases and expressions ('as a result', 'the reason is') and conjunctions ('when', 'after'). According to Halliday and Hasan (1976), there are four main groups of connectors (or four types of logical relationship):

1. *Temporal connectors*, e.g. 'first of all', 'then', 'next', 'before', 'after', 'immediately'.

   These express a temporal connection or relationship between parts of the text.

2. *Causal connectors*, e.g. 'because', 'in order to', 'therefore', 'so', 'as a result', consequently', 'the reason is'.

   These establish a causal connection, i.e. a relationship of cause and effect between parts of the text.

3. *Adversative connectors*, e.g. 'however', 'but', 'nevertheless', 'in spite of', 'on the other hand', 'yet', 'whereas', 'although'.

   These connectors indicate that what follows is in some sense opposed to, or contrasted with, what has gone before.

4. *Additive connectors,* e.g. 'and', 'also', 'in addition', 'moreover'.

   The connector here expresses a relationship of addition (or variation) between parts of the text.

See also *cohesion* and *conjunction*.

Connotation

Connotation refers to a procedure whereby a term, in addition to meanings allotted to it in a dictionary (denotative meanings), acquires additional significance resulting from the context in which it is applied. In this sense, the signifier 'white', apart from denoting a colour, might connote 'desire', 'absence', 'spirituality', 'death', etc., depending on the conditions of its application.

The distinction between connotative and denotative terms is frequently blurred.

See also *denotation.*

Content

According to the Danish linguist Louis Hjelmslev, there are two fundamental planes or levels of language, the plane of content and the plane of **expression**. These two levels are in relationship of presupposition. The level of expression relates to the domain of the signifier (sound, image, colour, etc.). The level of content, on the other hand, relates to the concept or idea (the signified) expressed by sound, image or colour, in other words, it concerns their semantic charge.

The expression *content analysis* is normally reserved to the domain of sociology and psychosociology. Content analysis in this case interprets a text (or a group of texts) from an a priori, categorical perspective directed at the mere quantification of data. Present tendencies, in semiotics at least, aim at transforming content analysis into discourse analysis.

See also *discourse* and *expression and content.*

Context

The term context designates any text that precedes or accompanies any specific signifying unit, and on which its meaning depends. Context, in this sense, can be explicit, implied or situational. When making a political speech, for instance, the *explicit* context might be documents on which the speaker bases his arguments; the *implied* context may be events or reasons that give rise to the speech while the *situational* context would refer to the set of circumstances under which it takes place and which also have a bearing on the meaning produced.

Context is one of the six elements or functions that figure in Jakobson's communication model. According to him any message, in order to make sense, must refer to a context understood by both sender (addresser) and receiver (addressee).

We also talk of *contextual* **semes** (or classemes). These are units of meaning, or bundles of meaning, which occur in both text and context. Thus, in their composition, contextual semes resemble sememes.

See also *classeme, seme* and *sememe*.

Contract

In general terms, a contract could be defined as the establishment of an intersubjective relationship which results in a modification of status (*l'être* and/or *le paraître*) affecting each of the subjects involved. In semiotic metalanguage, a narrative sequence starts with a contract/manipulation between a sender and a subject who undertakes to accomplish an action. The king contracts the knight to slay the dragon and offers him the hand of the princess in return. The knight, on the other hand, is prepared to offer his sword and his services in exchange for the king's promise to give him his daughter in marriage.

Before accepting this contract, however, an agreement of mutual trust must have been established. Otherwise what assurance would the knight have that the king will fulfil his pledge, or, for that matter, what assurance would the king possess that the knight is willing and able to execute his part of the bargain? In other words, without a firm belief in the truthfulness and reliability of the partner, the contract cannot become effective. This *fiduciary agreement*, which takes place on the enunciative level and precedes any actual or projected exchange of objects of value, is termed *contrat de véridiction*.

The fiduciary agreement, moreover, has two parts to it: a conclusion has to be reached as to whether one's partner is telling the truth, hiding something or downright lying, while the true value of the objects to be exchanged must also be ascertained and agreed. The activity involved in reaching consensus in these matters is cognitive: knowledge (*savoir-vrai*) is brought into play, coupled with persuasive doing on the one hand and on the other faith, acceptance (*croire-vrai*) as a result of interpretative doing. Both these manipulate in their own ways, but in the end agreement sanctioning the proceedings must be reached before any actual exchange can be settled.

Since this fiduciary agreement or enunciative contract is a prerequisite for any exchange of objects of value to become effective, it also applies to verbal transactions, that is, written texts or spoken utterances. Examples of this are to be found in normal conversation: the interlocutors' knowledge of each other, the images they project of their own credibility as well as the degree of acquaintance with the subject-matter under discussion affect the successful outcome of any communication.

The *contract/manipulation* refers to the first stage of the canonical narrative schema at which a sender transmits the modalities of desire or obligation to a receiver. Once the proposed modal status has been accepted, the contract is concluded and the receiver becomes a subject pursuing the quest that is to follow.

See also *canonical narrative schema*.

Contradiction

Contradiction is a logical component of the elementary structure of meaning. It is established as the result of the negation of one of the opposing terms, which is thereby rendered absent. The term 'life', for instance, is contradicted or negated by the term 'non-life'. Equally, the contradictory term of 'good' is 'non-good'.

The contradictory term thus produced *implies* the presence of the opposing term necessary to produce meaning. The term 'life' is contradicted by 'non-life', which in turn implies 'death', the latter being the opposing term in the semantic category of 'existence'.

The relationship can be outlined in a semiotic square:

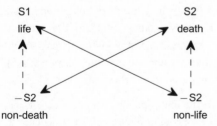

Here the term 'non-life' is in a relationship of contradiction to 'life' and of implication or complementarity to death.

See also *semiotic square*.

Contrary

A term can be described as contrary if its existence presupposes that of its opposite. 'Hot' and 'cold', 'high' and 'low', 'life' and 'death' are contraries, as each term is defined by its opposite which it therefore presumes to exist. In other words, to be contraries, two terms must possess a meaning in common or common denominator. Thus, 'high' and 'low' have the concept of 'verticality' in common, or 'hot' and 'cold' have 'temperature' as their common denominator.

See also *semantic category* and *semiotic square*.

Correlation

In semiotic analysis, correlation designates a link being established between different levels of meaning, in particular between the figurative (concrete) level and the thematic (abstract) level. In the works of William Blake, the figurative isotopy of the sea may, for example, be correlated with the abstract themes of freedom, love and unity; the isotopy of the city, on the other hand, may be correlated with themes of imprisonment, hatred or fragmentation.

Culture

Generally, the term culture designates the sum total of knowledge, attitudes and values which inform a society or characterize an individual. In this sense, culture is the product of human achievements and directly related to the human power of transformation. The arts belong to culture, as do thought products in general or, for that matter, anything produced by human beings.

Semiotic theory contrasts the concept of culture with that of *nature*. Thus when talking about eating habits in the sixteenth century, references to raw meat, fresh blood or killing animals would fall in the category nature, while allusions to cooking, recipes or table manners would be categorized as cultural behaviour.

In accordance with the anthropologist Claude Lévi-Strauss, semiotics posits that the opposing couple 'nature/culture' articulates the semantic category 'social life' whereas the couple 'life/death' characterizes the universe of the individual.

See also *nature*.

46

Débrayage/disengagement

In semiotic metalanguage *débrayage* refers to the act of projecting an utterance away from its enunciative source. The moment we start speaking we shift as it were into a new set of actorial, spatial and temporal co-ordinates constructed by our discourse. This 'change of gear' or 'disengagement' is called *débrayage*. The sentence 'The government faces an angry electorate' sets up an actor (the government), a space (the whole country, i.e. the seat of the electorate) and a time (the present, as indicated by the tense of the verb) which are separate or different from the actorial, spatial and temporal co-ordinates that apply to the speaker.

Débrayage also applies to the changeover between different discursive units or kinds of discourse as they, too, amount to a change of gear in the narration. If the expression 'Once upon a time ...' marks the initial *débrayage* of a discursive unit named fairy-tale, a dialogue, an interior monologue or a detailed description within the flow of the story would constitute a transformation or new 'shifting out' of the co-ordinates.

See also *embrayage* and *shifter*.

Decisive test

This is the stage of the canonical narrative schema at which the principal performance is enacted. It is the primary event (transformation) towards which the story has been leading. In other words, the decisive test corresponds to the moment where the object of the quest is at stake and the subject acquires (or fails to acquire) the desired goal. In the story of *Bluebeard*, the opening of the forbidden room may be considered the decisive test for the wife. In a general election, the electoral campaign represents the decisive test for the opposing parties, while the casting of votes is the decisive test for the voters.

See also *canonical narrative schema*.

Deixis

In semiotic analysis the term deixis can have two meanings:

Deixis

1. Deixis designates one of the fundamental dimensions of the **semiotic square**: through a process of implication it links one of the contrary terms with the contradictory of the other contrary term. There are, therefore, two deixes.

Let us take the example of the semiotic square of 'existence':

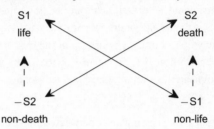

S1 (life) and −S2 (non-death) constitute one deixis. This is termed the *positive deixis*. S2 (death) and −S1 (non-life) constitute the second deixis, termed *negative deixis*. The terms positive and negative in this context are devoid of any axiological investment. This only appears as a result of the projection of the thymic category (euphoria versus dysphoria), that is, the category of feeling, onto the semiotic square.

2. Deixis is also used in a narrative as *deixis of reference*. In this context, temporal positions (now/then) or spatial positions (here/there) can be described as deixes of reference. Thus, for example, what is sometimes described as the 'time of the narrative' appears as a present identifiable with a 'then' deixis in relation to which a past and a future can be installed. In *Treasure Island* the search for the gold could be the deixis of reference in relation to which the preparatory events as well as the later moment of preserving the adventures in writing could be viewed as past and future.

Demonstrative reference

Demonstrative reference is a means by which cohesion is strengthened in a text. It can be expressed by determiners (this, that, these, those) or adverbs (here, then). These are used anaphorically to point backwards to a previously mentioned item or cataphorically to point forwards. The definite article 'the' can be considered as a particular type of demonstrative. Demonstratives can be used on their own or with nouns. Examples:

'We must keep him in bed and give him paracetemol three times a day as well as frequent hot drinks. If <u>that</u> fails, we must take him to the doctor.'

'In my days we took the matter more seriously. We had different ideas <u>then.</u>'

'<u>This</u> is what he wanted us to do: pick up the money, meet the men at the border, change vehicles and then head for Belfast.'

Denotation

Denotation designates the process of referring to the dictionary meanings of a word. It can be distinguished from connotation which relates to additional meanings resulting from the context in which the word is applied. The word 'rose', for example, denotes a flower or the shrub bearing it. In a particular context, however, the word 'rose' might connote love, or the House of Tudor.

See also *connotation*.

Descriptive

The term descriptive is normally used in connection with **values**. Descriptive values – in opposition to modal values – are attached to objects that can be consumed or hoarded (i.e. *objective* values) or to states of mind or feelings (i.e. *subjective* values). Bananas, for instance, represent descriptive values linked to objects, as do clothes, precious stones or cars. Smoking or listening to music, on the other hand, amount to descriptive values involving subjective feelings or pleasures.

Similarly, statements that deal with descriptive values are referred to as *descriptive statements*. Descriptive statements have to be distinguished from modal utterances that govern them. Thus the sentence 'The monkey wants the banana growing on the tree' contains two statements: a descriptive one ('the banana grows on the tree') and a modal one ('the monkey wants the banana').

See also *modal, modalization* and *object of value*.

Diachrony

The term diachrony designates the arrangement of time in a historical perspective. If we analyse the development of colonialism during the last two or three centuries, for example, our study will be diachronic.

Diachrony is opposed to *synchrony*, which refers to temporal coincidence of events. Thus, if synchrony describes different events all taking place at the same time, diachrony relates to occurrences arranged in sequence or on a vertical/historical axis.

Saussure introduced the dichotomy diachrony/synchrony for the description of language in a historical perspective (dealing with transformations of language over a period of time) and a synchronic perspective (concerning a contemporary language system). When describing abstract systems, however, any notion of time presents problems. Thus present-day linguistics operates within an atemporal or *achronic* framework.

See also *achrony* and *synchrony*.

Dialogue

The term dialogue denotes a discursive unit in speech structure. As a verbal exchange, it involves at least two interlocutors or participants who alternately take the parts of sender or receiver of a message. The designation interlocutor here refers to an instance performing a speech act. It has to be distinguished from the terms narrator and narratee, which describe the delegates of an enunciator/enunciatee of an utterance.

To give an example: Little Johnny wants a sweet. Little Johnny: 'I want a sweet.' Mother: 'Why do you want a sweet? You can't have one.' Little Johnny: 'But I want a sweet ...' In this instance, little Johnny and Mother are participants in an exchange of statements called a dialogue.

Reported dialogue often includes a framework stressing the speech act ('he said', 'she replied'). Additional information relative to the dialogue may also be offered ('nervously', 'with tears in her voice').

See also *communication model, enunciator/enunciatee* and *narrator/ narratee*.

Diegesis

Derived from the Greek, the term diegesis relates to 'the narrative aspect of discourse'. For the literary semiotician Gérard Genette, the term designates the narrated events or story, which he also names *histoire* as distinct from the level of narration, i.e. the telling of the story. In other words, the diegetic level of a narrative is that of the main events, whereas the 'higher' level at which they are told is extradiegetic (that is, standing outside the sphere of the main story).

Discourse

The term discourse denotes using language or talk generally, treating a subject verbally at length or making a speech.

According to Halliday, the term discourse designates a unit of language larger than a sentence and which is firmly rooted in a specific context. There are many different types of discourse under this heading, such as academic discourse, legal discourse, media discourse, etc. Each discourse type possesses its own characteristic linguistic features. This understanding of the term is generally accepted in discourse analysis.

In strictly semiotic terms, the word refers to the discursive level of meaning as opposed to the narrative level. A discourse is established through the interaction of two dimensions of language:

(1) the figurative dimension, relating to the representation of the natural world

(2) the thematic dimension, relating to the abstract values actualized in an utterance

In this sense, all manifestations of language can be envisaged as a discourse.

Discursive level

The discursive level relates to the process of putting the narrative structures into words, that is, of giving them figurative and linguistic shape. It is on this level that the actants/subjects, for example, are named and become actors, adopting thematic roles such as 'son', 'father' or 'soldier'; transformations enacted are arranged in chronological sequences and placed in a given space; the objects pursued are installed in systems of values which organize the utterance and determine the direction of desires and conflicts.

To analyse the discursive level of an utterance, we have to examine specific words and expressions or grammatical items/structures to discover their semiotic pertinence. Little Red Riding Hood is sent by her mother to take a cake to her grandmother. Thus she is placed in the position of an actant/subject pursuing a quest (narrative level). Her figurative description allots to this actant/subject the thematic role of child with the term 'little' alone establishing her vulnerability (discursive level). The story turns the wolf into an anti-subject (narrative level). The expression 'wolf' – a wild beast – and his figurative portrayal place him in the thematic role of a monster with the wish to harm (discursive level). Child and wolf and their conflicting narrative programmes here illustrate, for example, an underlying value-system which opposes in the shape of 'eating' versus 'being eaten', 'ogre' against 'victim' or 'evil' against 'good'.

There are no abstract formulas for the figurativization of texts or discursive trajectories, since most texts (particularly literary texts) are too complex to be reduced in this manner.

See also *actantial narrative schema*.

Discursive subject

The discursive subject is the subject through whose eyes places and events, etc., are being described. It may be internal (an actor in the story) or external (the position adopted by an imaginary observer). The discursive subject may or may not be identical with the narrative subject, that is, the subject of the main quest in the story. In *Treasure Island*, the discursive subject is Jim Hawkins, who is also a narrative subject in the quest to discover the treasure. In most fairy-tales, the discursive subject is an anonymous narrator who plays no part in the principal quest. In frame narratives, we usually have narrators who, while participating in the narrative they present, do not, or only minimally, function in the main story.

See also *narrative subject*.

Discursive units

In semiotics, the term discursive units covers what was traditionally called 'description', 'dialogue', 'narration', 'interior monologue', 'indirect speech', etc. These units are considered stages in the flow of a text and are analysed in their changing relationship with each other as well as with regard to the enunciative source as point of reference. Operations of *débrayage/embrayage* allow for the stages being shifted from one to the next.

See also *débrayage* and *embrayage*.

Discursivization

This relates to the syntactical organization of discursive elements which are expressed on the textual surface. In this sense, the procedures involved in discursivization are linked to the operations of *débrayage* and *embrayage*.

Basically, discursivization can be divided into three sub-components: actorialization, temporalization and spatialization. Together they set up the actorial, temporal and spatial framework in which narrative programmes can function. A narrative quest for love, for example, is put into words or discursivized in the story of Romeo and Juliet by installing actors (Romeo and Juliet), a place (Verona) and a time (long ago) on the textual surface.

See also *actorialization, spatialization* and *temporalization*.

Disjunction and conjunction

In semiotic theory the terms disjunction and **conjunction** articulate two possible relationships between a subject and an object. In the utterance 'John is poor', John, the subject, is in a relationship of disjunction with the object, wealth. In the utterance 'John has a great deal of money', on the other hand, the relationship between John and his object, wealth, is one of conjunction.

A narrative programme can be described as the transformation of a syntactical relationship between a subject and an object from one of disjunction to one of conjunction, or vice versa.

See also *narrative programme*.

Doing/*faire*

The term doing is synonymous with that of act (or action). The doing of a subject produces a transformation. In the sentence 'John buys a newspaper', the expression 'buys' represents John's doing. It transforms a situation of lack (having no newspaper) into one of reparation of lack (having a newspaper).

The expression **subject of doing** is employed to refer to a subject who in its relationship to an object, brings about a transformation. In the sentence 'John found a coin', John is the subject of doing because he has moved from a position of disjunction to one of conjunction with the object.

The subject of doing is to be distinguished from the subject of state whose relationship with an object remains unchanged. This kind of relationship is frequently expressed in verbs such as 'to be' or 'to have'. In the sentence 'John is poor', the position of John in relation to the object, poverty, does not vary. John, therefore, is a subject of state.

See also *subject of doing* and *subject of state*.

Donor

The term donor designates one of the seven spheres of action (and hence roles) which, according to Propp, make up the folk-tale. It describes 'the preparation for the transmission of a magical object and the provision of the hero with a magical object'. Other spheres of action include that of the villain, the dispatcher, the auxiliary hero, the false hero, the princess and her father, and finally the hero.

In narrative semiotics, the role of the donor – together with that of the auxiliary – is subsumed in the term 'helper'. The anti-donor, a term used by some semioticians, is related to the role of the opponent.

See also *helper* and *opponent*.

The term durative indicates the continuation of a process. It is frequently expressed in the use of the imperfect tense: 'He was reading a book'; 'We were having a great time'; 'She was a wonderful mother'.

A durative process is usually framed by an inchoative term marking its beginning and by a terminative term marking its end: 'In 1980 I moved to Paris. I lived there until last year.'

See also *inchoative* and *terminative*.

Dysphoria

This is the negative term of the thymic category, that is, the category that relates to the world of feeling and emotions. Dysphoria denotes unpleasant sensations and unhappiness which can be contrasted with their opposite, **euphoria**, the feeling of well-being or joy. In a text, the distinction euphoria versus dysphoria gives rise to an axiological system. An example of dysphoria would be: 'The fall of the democratic government and its replacement by a totalitarian regime was the cause of great misery.'

See also *aphoria*, *euphoria* and *thymic*.

Elementary utterance

The expression elementary utterance refers to the basic unit of meaning, which can be defined as a *relationship* between two actants. This relationship is expressed in a verb. The two actants, subject and object, for example, only exist in relationship to each other.

There are two kinds of elementary utterances:

(1) utterances of state, e.g. 'John is poor'; or 'The Queen owns Windsor Castle';

(2) utterances of doing, e.g. 'John reads the book', or 'The train arrives in the station'.

See also *actant, function* and *narrative programme.*

Ellipsis

Ellipsis occurs when some essential structural element is omitted from a sentence or clause and can only be recovered by referring to an element in the preceding text. In other words, the sentence can only be understood in conjunction with another utterance that supplies the missing element. For example:

A: I like the blue dress.   B: I prefer the green.
A: You work too hard.   B: So do you.

In both cases, the second sentence is incomprehensible without the first one.

Ellipsis is a common cohesive device in texts.

Embedding

The term embedding is sometimes used in semiotics to designate the insertion of a narrative (micro-narrative) into a larger narrative. It is synonymous with the term intercalation.

In Emily Brontë's *Wuthering Heights*, the story of Catherine and Heathcliff as told by the housekeeper is embedded within the story of the tenant Lockwood. Similarly, parables in the Bible story are examples of embedded or intercalated narratives.

Embrayage/engagement

If *débrayage* (disengagement) refers to a shifting away from the enunciative source and into a new set of actorial, spatial and temporal co-ordinates, *embrayage* (engagement) suspends this operation without annulling it, by re-injecting the enunciative presence. The statement, 'Yesterday the forecast said it would be raining in Scotland', for example, marks a *débrayage* by setting up an action, a time and a place different from that of the person who is speaking. The addition 'I went for a walk in the Scottish Hills and got wet', on the other hand, indicates an *embrayage* by making the presence of the actual speaker felt within the newly constructed set-up which it complements rather than cancels.

See also *débrayage* and *shifter*.

Emotion

In semiotic terms, emotion – like passion, which falls under the same heading – is described as a syntagmatic disposition of 'conditions of the soul/mind' (*états d'âme*). Thus we are dealing with states of being (*être*) as opposed to action/doing (*faire*). Cinderella is unhappy. Cinderella cries. There is often a close link between emotional states and preceding or subsequent action.

The connection, however, is even more complex at a stage prior to narrative action. The object of an emotion touches the subject, emotionally. It disturbs the subject, which is moved or disturbed by it. In this sense, an action (*faire*) takes place as a result of which the subject is unbalanced, it is no longer what it was before and even its behaviour may be altered. A gentle, loving husband turns jealous and kills his wife. Joy, happiness give strength to perform deeds one never dreamt of. Emotion is therefore also linked to a micro-transformation, albeit on the level of being (*être*), that precedes the macro-narrative.

See also *semiotics of passion*.

Enunciative subject

In semiotic analysis we distinguish between the *enunciator* of an utterance and the *enunciatee* to whom it is addressed. In conversation, two interlocutors take part in an intersubjective exchange, in turn advancing propositions and accepting or rejecting them. On the surface level, therefore, enunciator and enunciatee adopt distinctly different positions: one asking to be believed, the other conferring belief or withholding it. On a deeper level, however, the different participants in the exchange come together in one syncretic figure representing the enunciative performance in its entirety. It is in this context that we talk of the subject of enunciation, or the enunciative subject, which comprises both proposition and acceptance or rejection, like two sides of a whole glued by their fiduciary relation. On the discursive level, this unity is illustrated by, for instance, the syncretism manifest in the expression 'He believed in himself'.

See also *enunciator/enunciatee* and *epistemological subject*.

Enunciator/enunciatee

The term enunciator refers to the instance initiating a speech act. S/he is the author/sender of a message addressed to an enunciatee or receiver.

The enunciator has to be distinguished from the narrator of a written text or verbal communication. The narrator is in fact a construct, an actant to whom the enunciator – by means of the procedure of *débrayage* – has delegated his/her voice. The 'I' in an utterance, therefore, is not identical with the enunciator but a verbal simulacrum of a narrative presence. Correspondingly, the real enunciatee/receiver of the message is represented in a text by an actant/delegate, the narratee. The latter may, or may not, be present on the discursive level with the mention 'you'.

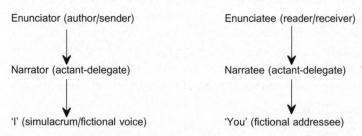

The author Robert Louis Stevenson is the enunciator of the novel *Treasure Island*. Stevenson delegates his voice to a narrating instance, here finding expression in the narrative actant Jim Hawkins. The enunciatee of the novel, on the other hand, the reading public, finds its delegate in the construction of a fictional narratee (model audience) represented in the text by the simulacra of the gentlemen for whom the account is supposedly written.

See also *narrator/narratee*.

Episteme

The term episteme comes from the Greek and refers to knowledge, a system of understanding. Following Michel Foucault, it has also become accepted as signifying the body of ideas which shape the perception of knowledge at a particular period.

In semiotic theory, episteme has two definitions. Firstly, the term can designate the hierarchical organization of different semiotic systems capable of generating all possible manifestations covered by these systems within a given culture. Greimas, for example, attempted to construct an episteme by hierarchically organizing semiotic systems of sexual, economic and socio-matrimonial relations within the traditional French cultural space.

Secondly, episteme can be defined as a form of cultural meta-semiotics in the sense that it describes the attitude taken by a socio-cultural community towards its own signs. Thus in medieval culture, for instance, signs were essentially metonymic, expressing subjacent wholeness. In eighteenth-century French culture, on the other hand, signs were 'natural', simply denoting objects.

Epistemic modalities

The term epistemic relates to knowledge, its theory or scientific study, and the modalities connected involve certainty/uncertainty and probability/improbability.

In semiotic terms, epistemic modalities form part of the competence needed by an enunciatee to evaluate a proposition. In order to establish an enunciative contract (implicit or explicit), an enunciator attempts to persuade (*faire croire*) the enunciatee, who, for his/her part, seals his/her own interpretative doing with an epistemic judgement, that is, with either believing (*croire*) the enunciator or doubting (*ne pas croire*) his/her statements. If I accept the weather forecast and believe that tomorrow the sun will shine, I have judged the prognosis believable.

Epistemic modalities are also part of the necessary competence for a sender-adjudicator to carry out its function in the canonical narrative schema. The epistemic judgement in this instance refers to the assessment of the narrative subject's performance being in accordance with the initial contract. It also relates to cognitive sanction in that it distributes belief or disbelief in statements made within a narrative. The king, for example, who has asked the knight to slay the dragon in return for the hand of his daughter, may not believe (negative epistemic judgement) that the task has been accomplished when the knight returns. On the other hand, he may be persuaded to acknowledge the deed (positive epistemic judgement) when seeing the monster's cut-off heads, or listening to an eyewitness account.

Scientific discourse in particular is characterized by a surfeit of epistemic modalization which appears to take the place of verifying procedures. The same goes for the experimental sciences and all discourse whose hypotheses are difficult to verify.

See also *certainty* and *uncertainty*.

Epistemological subject

The epistemological subject or true subject of enunciation is the underlying voice in a text giving expression to a system of knowlege, ideology, or 'vision of the world'. It is not necessarily the voice of the narrator. The profile of an epistemological subject emerges through an examination of the language and structures of a text, for example, through a study of the spatial element.

Epistemology

In general terms, epistemology denotes the theory or science of the method or grounds of knowledge. In other words, epistemology studies the ways in which a science, for example, erects its axioms and constructs knowledge.

Semiotic theory applies the term epistemology to the analysis of the cognitive dimension not only of scientific discourse but all discourse since all discourse proposes – implicitly or explicitly – an approach to and a theory of knowledge.

See also *cognitive*.

Euphoria

This is the positive term of the thymic category relating to the world of feeling and emotions. Euphoria denotes pleasant sensations and joy and is opposed to the negative term dysphoria which signifies unpleasant feelings and unhappiness. In a text, the distinction euphoria versus dysphoria gives rise to an axiological sytem. An example of euphoria is: 'When Mary passed the examination, she felt happy'. Dysphoria is illustrated by: 'He was horrified by the enormity of the crime.'

See also *aphoria, dysphoria* and *thymic.*

Evaluative

Evaluative terms, such as 'good', 'bad', 'beautiful' or 'nice', refer to the instance of enunciation and imply a judgement or particular attitude on the part of the speaker. Their use renders an utterance more subjective.

Evaluative terms frequently take the form of adjectives or adverbs. Examples: I had a nice evening. He has done the work very badly.

The absence of evaluative terms gives an impression of greater objectivity. It is, therefore, a feature of scientific or legal discourse.

Expression and content

According to Hjelmslev, there are two fundamental planes or levels of language, the *plane of expression* and the *plane of content*. These two planes correspond to Saussure's distinction between the signifier (expression) and the signified (content). They are in a relationship of reciprocal presupposition. The level of expression relates to the domain of sound (music, the spoken word), to that of shape or colour or line (graphic icons or images), to that of movement or gestures. The level of content, on the other hand, relates to the concept or idea expressed by these sounds or icons, in other words, it concerns their semantic charge. In our traffic light system, for example, the colours and their spatial layout – green, amber, red – belong to the level of expression. Their significance – green = go, red = stop – belongs to the level of content.

Hjelmslev, however, defines the two planes of language even further:

Expression and content	*The level of expression.* The level of expression can itself be subdivided into two components, the **substance** of expression and the **form** of expression. Music and the spoken word, for instance, have the same substance of expression: sound. Their form or organization, however, differs: language uses the linguistic system; music employs its own arrangements of opposition and metre. The same applies to the world of colour and shape as a means of expression: the substances – painting, photography, drawing – all take distinctive forms in the way they are organized and applied.

The level of content. This may also be subdivided into the **substance** of content and the **form** of content. The substance of content has been described as an original amorphous continuum of meaning. Hjelmslev gives the example of the general idea of sibling relationship (*fraternité*) considered as a type of nebula. This substance of content takes different forms in different cultures. French (and English), for example, possess the two distinct terms: brother and sister. Hungarian has, in addition, separate terms for younger or older brother or sister, etc. The Mayan language, on the other hand, does not differentiate between brother and sister at all: one term – *sudara* – is used to cover them both.

It must be remembered that the substance of content can only be apprehended through its form: the substance is presupposed but beyond the reach of linguistic investigation. Hjelmslev's concept of language, therefore, supports Saussure's claim that language is a form and not a substance.

See also *signifier and signified.*

Expressive function

If a communication is focusing on the addresser (sender) of the message, calling attention to his/her feelings, beliefs or emotions, then it is the expressive (or emotive) function that dominates. The expressive function is indicated in several ways:

(1) through the use of exclamation marks and interjections.

(2) through the use of modalization, that is, linguistic devices that point to the presence of a narrator, drawing our attention to the subjective source of an utterance. The two principal forms here are:

- the use of emotive or evaluative terms (expressing judgement) that reveal the presence of a narrator: 'The father had forgotten the <u>poor</u> girl. She was lying awake and <u>unhappy</u>. In the midst of friends ... she was <u>alone</u>' (W. M. Thackeray, *Vanity Fair*).

Expressive function

- the use of terms that nuance or rectify a statement such as 'seem', 'appear', 'perhaps', 'undoubtedly', 'certainly', etc. 'One would <u>certainly</u> <u>suppose</u> her to be further on in life than her seventeenth year – <u>perhaps</u> because of the slow, resigned sadness of the glance ... <u>perhaps</u> because ...' (George Eliot, *The Mill on the Floss*).

Dominance of the expressive function in a text does not preclude the other speech functions being present to varying degrees.

See also *communication model*.

F

Figurative

Figurative elements are those elements in a text that correspond to the physical world and can be apprehended by the five senses (vision, touch, taste, hearing and smell). They are essential ingredients in the construction of a reality effect or illusion of a real world.

Figurative elements operate on the surface level of a text, creating, for example, an impression of time, of place or of character. They should be contrasted with the abstract or conceptual component that belongs to the deep level. In the sentence 'I remember him as if it were yesterday, a tall, strong, heavy nut-brown man', the second part is predominantly figurative while 'remember' and 'yesterday' are abstract notions.

See also *figure*.

Figurativization

Figurativization refers to the process whereby an enunciator invests abstract values in his discourse with figurative shape. When telling the story of a man wishing to be seen to possess power, for example, the enunciator might choose a powerful car as figurative manifestation of his desire to dominate. Or he might elaborate on how the man acquired the car of his dreams and how he enjoyed his neighbours' or friends' recognition of the power the object 'car' represented.

See also *figurative* and *figure*.

Figure

In semiotic terms, figure refers to the expression of abstract values on the figurative level of discourse. The abstract value 'life', for example, might take shape on the discursive level in the figure of a newly born baby, a growing plant or a flowing river.

See also *figurativization*.

Focalization

The term focalization refers to the angle of vision or position of the observer. It relates to the fundamental question: through whose eyes is the story being told, from whose point of view? There are two principal categories of focalization:

(a) *internal focalization*, in which events are described as they appear through the eyes of an actor in the story. Examples would be Meursault's account in Albert Camus's novel *L'Etranger*, or the narrator in *A la recherche du temps perdu* by Marcel Proust.

(b) *external focalization*, in which events are described as they appear through the eyes of an external observer/narrator who is not an actor in the story. This is a characteristic of much of nineteenth-century realist or naturalist fiction such as the novels of George Eliot, Honoré de Balzac or Emile Zola.

See also *focalizer*.

Focalizer

The term focalizer refers to the subject through whose eyes events are being described. It is synonymous with the term observer.

See also *focalization*.

Form

In semiotic theory, the term form is opposed to that of *matter* which it 'informs' by 'forming' the recognizable object. Thus the 'form' of any object guarantees its permanence and its identity. An earthenware cup becomes recognizable as a cup only after the clay from which it is has been taken assumes the form of a cup. Mountains aren't mountains until the original magma shapes itself into a form called 'mountains'.

Saussure defined language as a form composed of two substances. Neither all 'physical', nor totally 'psychological', it is the place where these components converge. As a result, Saussure believed language to be a signifying structure.

The Saussurian affirmation is developed further by Hjelmslev, who postulates the existence of a distinct form for each of the two levels of language: both *content* and *expression* of language are subdivided into their own distinctive substance and form. Accordingly, when investigating language, the form of the expression as well as the form of the content need to be recognized and analysed separately.

See also *expression and content, matter* and *substance*.

Function

In linguistics and in semiotics, the term function has at least three applications: it is used in an instrumental and utilitarian sense; with syntactical meaning; and in a logico-mathematical sense.

1. For the linguist A. Martinet, the predominant function of language is to communicate. Language has a *useful function* as instrument in social interaction.

2. The term function in a *syntactical* context refers firstly to parts played by certain elements in a sentence (subject, object, predicate). The linguist E. Benveniste uses the concept function as a necessary element to define a structure in language (all its constituent parts fulfil a function). Jakobson, for his part, employs the term function to designate the six elements that make up the speech act (expressive, conative, referential, poetic, meta-lingual and phatic). Finally, Propp makes use of the term function to describe syntagmatic units in folk-tales which are common to all stories.

3. Hjelmslev defines the term in a *logico-mathematical* sense, considering function to designate 'the relation between two variables'. Semiotics reserves the term function for the definition of the relationship between two actants. This relationship is expressed in the verb of the elementary utterance. Any other narrative functions, subject or object for example, are simply named actants.

Semiotic function, according to Hjelmslev, designates the relationship in language between the form of expression and that of content.

See also *actant, communication model, elementary utterance, Propp* and *syntax.*

Generative trajectory

The term generative trajectory designates the process whereby meaning is constructed. It is based on the notion of a hierarchy of meaning reflecting the fundamental division between deep and surface structures and between abstract and concrete. According to this model, complex structures derive from simple structures in a process of ever-greater enrichment of meaning.

The starting point (*ab quo*) of the generative trajectory is the deep abstract level associated with Greimas's elementary structure of meaning and the semiotic square. It is from this level that the narrative level is generated which in turn gives rise to the discursive level. We may take the example of the abstract category life versus death situated on the deep level. On the narrative level these values could be articulated in terms of narrative programmes (conjunction and disjunction) and in relationship to an actantial subject. Life, for example, may be the object of a quest. On the discursive level these values are articulated in their most concrete form, and they acquire a figurative shape. Life could be expressed in the figure of light, whereas death could be conveyed in that of darkness.

Each of the three levels of meaning contains two components, a syntactic component and a semantic component. The semantic component relates to the semantic content (signified) of individual words and syntagms which the syntactic component articulates and structures on each of the different levels of signification.

See also *semantics* and *syntax*.

Genre

Referring originally to different styles of literary discourse (sonnets, tragedies, romances etc.), the term genre has been widened to include all types of oral or written communication such as a casual conversation, a recipe, an advert or a political address. Different genres are characterized by a particular structure, by grammatical forms or special turns of phrases that reflect the communicative purpose of the genre in question. A sermon, for example, has its own distinctive characteristics that would differentiate it from a job interview, a shopping list or a mail-order catalogue. In this sense, the term genre has currently the same meaning as 'discourse type'.

Gift

The term gift describes a discursive figure relating to the communication of objects of value. It refers to a transformation resulting from an attribution (the acquiring of an object) or a renunciation (the deprivation of an object). In other words, as a consequence of a gift, the subject of state (S2) may:

(1) be in possession of an object of value following the act of a subject of doing (S1) other than itself. This is known as *transitive conjunction*. Example: 'Peter gave Paul the ten-pound note he had found.'

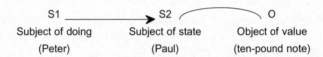

	S1		S2		O
	Subject of doing		Subject of state		Object of value
	(Peter)		(Paul)		(ten-pound note)

(2) deprive itself of an object of value. This act is known as *reflexive disjunction*. Example: 'Paul gave his life for his country.'

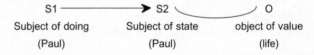

	S1		S2		O
	Subject of doing		Subject of state		object of value
	(Paul)		(Paul)		(life)

See also *attribution*.

Glorifying test

This is the stage of judgement or sanction in a narrative quest. It corresponds to those episodes where the outcome of an event is revealed. The decisive test has either succeeded or failed, the heroine/hero is acclaimed or punished, the act is deemed good or evil. It is the point at which the performance is interpreted either by the narrator or by an actor in the story. The instance doing the interpreting is known as the sender-adjudicator. S/he judges whether the performance of the subject is in accordance with the original set of values established by the first sender (also known as mandating sender) and whether the contract has been fulfilled or not. In traditional fairy-tales the stage of sanction is frequently enacted in the figure of marriage: the father may reward the hero for his achievements (killing the dragon, for example) by giving him his daughter's hand in marriage.

See also *canonical narrative schema*.

The term grammar designates the part of language study that deals with the forms of words, their organization in clauses and sentences, and the rules that govern structures and operations. There are two main components of grammar: morphology (the study of words) and syntax (their arrangement in sentences).

Semiotic theory has adopted the term grammar for the description of semio-narrative structures of signification. Correspondingly, semiotic grammar has two basic components applicable to different levels of signification: (1) *semantics* studying units of meaning and states of being, and (2) *syntax* studying their relationships, organization and transformation.

See also *morphology, semantics* and *syntax*.

Having-to-be

See *alethic modalities*.

Having-to-do

This modal structure governs utterances of doing (action). Terms expressing obligation or prescription, prohibition, permission and optionality relate to this category, which can be projected onto the following semiotic square:

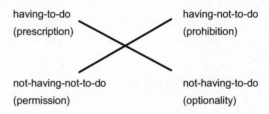

having-to-do   having-not-to-do
(prescription)   (prohibition)

not-having-not-to-do   not-having-to-do
(permission)   (optionality)

Example: 'Mary felt she had to go (*obligation*) to France the following Wednesday to attend the conference even though it was strictly forbidden (*having-not-to-do*) to take time off for any reason. She did not, therefore, ask permission (*not-having-not-to-do*) to go: it would simply be up to the management (*not-having-to-do*) whether they sacked her or not.'

See also *alethic modalities*.

Helper

Any actant that aids the subject in its quest is known as a helper. In the fairy-tale *Cinderella*, the fairy godmother and the coach function as helpers in Cinderella's quest to go to the ball. During a general strike, pickets or newspaper articles may function as actant/helpers depending on the point of view.

Hermeneutics

The term hermeneutics generally designates the interpretation of philosophical and religious texts. It brings into play the relation of the text to the referent and is particularly concerned with extra-linguistic data such as the conditions of production or reception of the texts. Its emphasis, therefore, is on socio-historic context including contemporary interpretations.

Hero

In semiotic theory, the term hero designates the subject actant of a narrative trajectory (or quest) once it has come into possession of a certain competence, that is, of a being-able-to-do and/or knowing-how-to-do. A pilot who sets off to fly around the world in a hot-air balloon must possess the necessary skill and equipment: s/he can then be termed a hero.

An *actualized* hero is a hero who is in possession of this competence but who has not yet passed to the stage of performance. It can be distinguished from the *realized* hero who is in possession of the object of the quest. In our example, the hero is actualized in the act of flying. If the balloon succeeds in going round the world, then the hero can be described as realized.

In a more conventional meaning of a word, especially in oral and classical works, the term hero is endowed with euphoric connotations and is opposed to that of villain (the dysphoric or nasty).

See also *actualization* and *realization*.

Heterotopic space

The term heterotopic space designates those places whose mention in a story precedes or follows the narrative transformation. They are external, therefore, to the events that make up the pivot of the story. In *Treasure Island*, Jim Hawkins's home (from which he sets out and to which he returns after finding the treasure) constitutes a heterotopic space. In *Jack and the Beanstalk*, Jack's home likewise represents a heterotopic space.

See also *topic space* and *utopic space*.

Hierarchy

In semiotic theory, hierarchy appears as the organizing principle of the elementary structure of meaning. The two terms in opposition that are essential for the production of meaning are thus considered hierarchically inferior to their common denominator or the category as a totality. The category 'emotion', for example, may be considered as hierarchically superior to its component parts in a text, say, to the terms of 'love' versus 'hatred'.

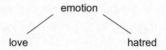

See also *semantic category*.

Homologation

In general terms, homologation designates a process of correlation between different levels of meaning. In a poetic text, the figure of the bird could be homologized with the semes of 'high' and of 'life', for example, whereas the figure of the rat could be homologized with those of 'low' and of 'death'.

See also *correlation*.

Hypotactic

The term hypotactic expresses the relation of a whole to its parts and vice versa. Greimas gives the following example from Maupassant's short story *Two Friends*: 'Paris was blockaded, famished, a death rattle in her throat. The sparrows rarely appeared on the roofs, and even the sewers were being emptied of their regular tenants.' Here the relationship between Paris and her 'roofs' and 'sewers' is hypotactic.

For Hjelmslev the term hypotactic designates the logical relation between a presupposed term and a presupposing term. In the above example, 'roofs' and 'sewers' presuppose Paris.

Icon

In the semiotics of the American philosopher C. S. Peirce, an icon is a sign which resembles the object it signifies. A portrait, for example, is an icon because it resembles the subject represented. A diagram of a house is the icon of a house.

See also *index* and *symbol.*

Iconicity

The term iconicity means resemblance to 'reality', to the natural world outside the text. Its meaning is similar to that of referential impression or illusion. Iconization is the procedure whereby this impression of the referential world is produced and sustained. The evocation of London in Charles Dickens's novels is an example of iconization.

The distanciation (alienation) technique, on the other hand, that characterizes Brecht's theatre is a form of de-iconization.

Identity

The notion of identity is opposed to that of otherness and cannot be defined in any other way. In fact, the terms 'identity' and 'otherness' are interdefinable by relationship of presupposition. For instance, in a biographical novel the reader recognizes the protagonist's identity by setting it off against the 'otherness' of other characters. Moreover, if the story is to make sense, changes provoked by action and plot do not affect the basic identity of actors. Thus identity can also be seen as permanence in opposition to transformation.

Finally, the couple 'identity' and 'otherness' and their relationship form an essential basis for the elementary structure of signification or semiotic square.

See also *semiotic square.*

Ideology

Strictly speaking, the term ideology designates the science of ideas. It is commonly employed, however, to refer to a body of ideas and values characteristic of an individual, a society or a school of thought. We talk of the Marxist ideology or a capitalist ideology, for example, or the ideology of the upper classes.

Because of the richness and ambiguities of terms related to value, semiotic theory distinguishes two basic organizing principles governing their expression: on the one hand there are **systems** of value that are arranged on a *paradigmatic* axis signifying either by equivalence or opposition. For example, in such a system 'wealth' signifies in opposition to 'poverty' but on an equivalent level with 'opulence' or 'riches'. The term axiology has been reserved for these paradigmatic value systems.

The term ideology, on the other hand, is used to describe the *syntagmatic* arrangement of values, that is their **actualization** in a quest. Subjects desire values which become objects of quests. The values themselves, of course, form part of axiological systems. Their selection and setting up as goals, however, define ideology. Once a quest is realized, we no longer talk of ideology. In other words, the notion of ideology contains a permanent quest as reflected in the actantial structure of its discourse. To offer an example: considering the Christian faith an ideology, we find the Bible stories, again and again, presenting moral values as goals to be achieved but not yet attained.

See also *actualization* and *axiology.*

Idiolect

The term idiolect refers to an individual person's specific use of language or semiotic activity. An idiolect contains individual variations from the norm. Such variations must not be too excessive or else communication will be jeopardized.

See also *sociolect.*

Illocutionary act

According to the speech act theory (J. L. Austin) an illocutionary act is an utterance that involves performing an act. In other words, when I say something, I am not only describing reality, my words are also having a direct effect on this reality. For instance, the speaker performs the act of promising by saying 'I promise'. Illocutionary acts can take the form of threats, warnings, questions, commands or giving advice.

See also *performative* and *perlocutionary act*.

Illusion

On the semiotic square of veridiction, the term illusion subsumes the complementary terms of 'seeming' and 'non-being' which are located on the negative pole or deixis.

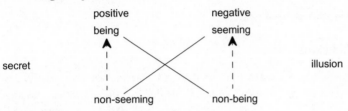

See also *deixis* and *veridiction*.

Immanence and manifestation

Immanent structures are those semantic and logical structures that are situated at the deep level of a text. They can be contrasted with the structures or elements that are manifest on the linguistic surface, that is, with the actual words, pictures or sounds which constitute the text. Immanent structures can be deduced from an examination of elements perceptible on the textual surface.

The relationship between immanence and manifestation is similar to that between content and expression.

See also *expression and content*.

Inchoative

An inchoative term is an aspectual term describing the beginning of a process. It indicates that a transformation has taken place and is frequently conveyed through the use of the simple past (the preterite or perfect tense in French), or the narrative present: 'He came into the room'; 'He comes into the room'.

The end of a process, on the other hand, is indicated in the use of a *terminative* term: 'He left the room'.

See also *durative* and *terminative*.

Index

In Peirce's semiotics, an index is a sign that is physically linked to, or affected by, its object. The relationship between sign and object, or signifier and signified, may be causal or sequential. Examples given by Peirce are a weathercock, a barometer and a sundial. A knock at the door indicating that there is someone at the door is another example of a sign seen as an index. Pointing my finger at a dog is the index of a dog. A high temperature may be seen as an index of illness.

See also *icon* and *symbol*.

Individual

An actant is termed individual to mark a contrast with a collective actant defined as a collection of individuals endowed with a narrative role. In Zola's *Germinal*, the miners represent a collective actant whereas Etienne Lantier is an individual actant.

The term individual is also used to describe a semantic universe characterized by the category life/death. The James Bond films would be an example of such a universe.

See also *collective*.

Interoceptive/exteroceptive

Interoceptive doing designates actions that are *non-figurative*, that is, actions that take place inside the mind and relate to an internal world, such as thinking, remembering or feeling. The term can be contrasted with that of exteroceptive doing. This designates actions that are concrete and relate to the external physical world such as seeing, eating, jumping, etc.

Interpretation

Interpretation involves the operations of recognition and identification. 'Re'-cognition or 're'-discovery, in this sense – contrary to acquiring knowledge – is an act of comparing a proposition with what is already known. Recognition as comparison, furthermore, necessarily comprises identifying, in any particular utterance, all or parts of a truth one already possesses. Interpreting any statement means weighing what one already knows to be true against what is being proposed and deciding in the light of this on its meaning and accuracy. For instance, political propaganda anticipates the general public's interpretation being based on comparison of facts personally known to be true (unemployment, rising prices) with those advertised as being correct.

The same applies to the interpretation of literary texts. The story of *Cinderella*, for example, draws on our knowledge of other fairy-tales as well as our familiarity with human behaviour in general, love, jealousy, etc. All this helps to identify essential moments in the story which explain its meaning.

Isotopy

The term isotopy refers to recurring semic categories whose presence ensures sustained meaning in the flow of a text. Isotopies thus provide continuity in the deciphering of, for example, a narrative. Their absence, on the other hand, produces an effect of semantic dislocation which may, of course, be what the author intends to achieve. To give an example: frequent reference in a text to times of day, dawn or dusk, to age or eternity coupled with expressions stressing always or never, or detailed dates or pronounced indication of tenses, can be seen as establishing the isotopy of 'time'.

In critical metalanguage, isotopy replaces the traditional terms 'theme' and 'motif'. Isotopies are to be found on the figurative level, allowing for the assembling of semantic fields perceptible on the textual surface; or, by constant repetition of the same lexeme for example, they amount to semantic specification. On the abstract level, isotopies reveal common denominators which structure the deep level of meaning.

Iterative

The term iterative signifies telling once what 'happened' many times. For instance: 'Every night I went to bed at ten o'clock.'

See also *repeated event* and *singular*.

K

Knowing-how-to-do

The modality of knowing-how-to-do constitutes a key component of narrative competence. In order for the subject to be fully qualified and proceed to the decisive test, it must acquire

> (a) the modality of being-able-to-do and/or (b) the modality of knowing-how-to-do

If the object of a quest is to pass an examination with honours, then the candidate will need to acquire the necessary knowledge and skills (= knowing-how-to-do) to achieve this goal. If the object is winning a shooting competition, there is no point in possessing a gun and presenting oneself at the appointed place and time without knowing-how-to-shoot.

These modalities of knowing-how-to-do and being-able-to-do are known as the actualizing modalities. They can be contrasted on the one hand with the virtualizing modalities (wanting-to-do and/or having-to-do) where the subject is established, and on the other with the realizing modalities ('being' and 'doing') where the subject is realized.

See also *canonical narrative schema* and *modalization*.

Lack

The term lack expresses a state of disjunction between a subject and an object. In abstract terms this is represented thus:

The state of disjunction, the sense of a loss, of something missing is frequently the trigger for the global narrative programme known as the quest. Most stories and indeed human action in general spring from an essential dissatisfaction with the world.

The lack is eliminated by means of a transformation bringing about a conjunction of subject and object. This transformation corresponds to the decisive test or performance.

The term 'lack' was originally coined by Propp, for whom it is closely associated with the 'misdeed' of the villain. It is this misdeed that triggers the quest whose ultimate aim is to remedy a lack and rectify a misdeed.

See also *actantial narrative schema* and *canonical narrative schema*.

Language

The term language designates any signifying whole (system) be it verbal, musical, visual, gestural etc. We speak of a language of architecture, a language of music or a language of landscape, to mention just a few examples. A language must necessarily bring into play the relationship signifier/signified (Saussure) or (in Hjelmslev's terminology) expression and content. To take the language of traffic lights for instance: the colours green-amber-red in their respective positions and order constitute the signifiers, whereas the signifieds are go-be careful-stop. In other words, a language must always consist of a form and a content, the two facets being deemed inseparable.

Referring to the spoken language (English, French, Italian, etc.), Saussure makes the distinction between *langue* and *parole*. He uses the term *langue* to denote the abstract set of rules and conventions underlying a given language, whereas *parole* designates the concrete manner in which each individual speaker makes use of this system.

See also *expression and content* and *signifier and signified*.

Language act

According to the theories of J. R. Searle all linguistic utterances possess an illocutionary power, that is, they not only communicate a content (ideas etc.) but also establish a particular relationship – one of intentionality – between enunciator (addresser) and enunciatee (addressee). An utterance, for example, could be an order, a promise, a request, etc., that is, it could be any from a variety of language acts.

Examples: 'It is raining' is an act of affirmation on the part of the enunciator. 'Please do not leave litter on the lawn' – this is a request verging on a command.

See also *illocutionary act* and *perlocutionary act.*

Lexeme

A lexeme represents the totality of possible or virtual meanings attached to a particular word. Only a select number of these meanings will be actualized in a discourse.

In general usage, the term lexeme has the same meaning as 'word'. 'Apple', for example, is a lexeme/word whose figurative or metaphorical meaning will be actualized in the context of a discursive unit. We call the actualized units of meaning a sememe.

See also *sememe.*

Lexia

For B. Pottier the term lexia designates fundamental lexical units (units of meaning). These units can be grouped into three categories:

(a) simple lexias: these are simple lexemes such as 'cat', 'dog', and affixed lexemes such as 'unconstitutional'.

(b) compound lexias: these are fixed syntagmes such as 'horse-power', 'shoe-tree', etc.

(c) complex lexias: these are expressions such as 'to take into account', 'to take care of'.

Lexical cohesion

Lexical cohesion occurs when two (or more) words in a text are semantically related, that is, they are related in terms of their meaning or content. Common devices of lexical cohesion are: pronouns, repetition, collocations and synonyms. An example of repetition would be 'I bought some books because books are my passion'. Collocation, on the other hand, is illustrated by a sentence such as 'His body burnt with the fire of his passion'. The words 'fire' and 'burnt' are both used to express passion.

See also *cohesion* and *collocation.*

Lexical field

A lexical field is formed by grouping together words under one general umbrella term. 'Apple', 'banana', 'strawberry', etc. would all form part of a lexical field headed 'fruit'.

See also *semantic field.*

Lexicology

The term lexicology designates the scientific study of words. Until semantics was recognized as an autonomous branch of science, lexicology was the only area in linguistics to study problems relating to the meaning of words.

See also *lexeme, lexical field* and *semantics.*

Life/death

Life is the positive term of the life/death category whose semantic axis (common denominator of meaning) can be called existence. The category life/death constitutes a thematic elementary structure and can be regarded as universal. It gives rise to the following semiotic square:

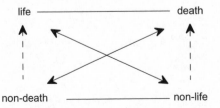

Life/death

The category life/death can be connoted by the thymic category. Very frequently, the positive and negative terms are coupled, that is, life + euphoric; death + dysphoric. However, this is not always the case: for someone about to commit suicide, life equals dysphoria.

See also *semiotic square*.

Listener

Like the term reader, the listener designates the receiver of a verbal communication, in this case of an oral nature. In semiotics, the more general term enunciatee is preferred.

See also *enunciator/enunciatee*.

Manifestation

See *immanence and manifestation*.

Matter

In semiotic theory, the term matter denotes the formless raw material which allows immanent form to manifest itself. Hjelmslev employs indiscriminately the term matter and the term purport when talking of 'manifestation' of language on both the level of expression and that of content.

See also *form* and *immanence and manifestation*.

Metalanguage

A metalanguage is a language that is unique to a particular branch of knowledge. It is composed of the specialized concepts or terminology needed to define the discipline. Medicine, for example, has its own metalanguage, as does the science of law, literature, art, etc. Semiotics itself is a metalanguage, in other words, the term refers to the language or concepts that define the manner meaning is produced.

The meanings of terms used in a metalanguage tend to be stable, i.e. independent (as far as possible) of any specific context.

Metalingual function

If a communication is orientated towards the code used – lexical meaning in a verbal text or number symbolism in mathematical discourse, for instance – then it is the metalingual function that dominates. In general, the purpose of the metalingual function is to check that the same code is being used by both parties, that they understand each other. Utterances such as 'in other words', 'do you understand?', 'what I mean to say' are illustrative of this function. Dictionaries are a good example of the metalingual function dominating a text.

Dominance of the metalingual function in a text does not preclude the other speech functions being present to varying degrees.

See also *communication model*.

Metaphor

The term metaphor designates the procedure by which a given sentential unit is substituted for another, thereby transforming its original semantic charge. In other words, a substitute name or descriptive expression is transferred to some object/person to which it is not literally applicable: 'pilgrimage', for instance, is employed instead of 'life', 'burning fire' to express the notion 'love', 'lamb' to describe a child, etc.

See also *metonymy*.

Metasemiotics

The term metasemiotics refers to the theory of meaning produced on a second or higher level of signification. Any utterance which can be semiotically investigated may also cause effects that cannot be explained by analysing linguistic data. For instance: Why do we believe someone's words to be true when they themselves offer no guarantee for such trust? What makes us understand the opening passage of a book as fiction or documentary account, if there is no firm verbal indication as to which way it is to be taken?

According to Hjelmslev, there are two basic types of metasemiotics: a scientific one and a non-scientific one. Non-scientific metasemiotics falls within the domain of philosophy, ontology and even ethics. It concerns, in fact, a fiduciary agreement between an enunciator and an enunciatee which, in everyday life, cannot be analysed in terms of objective science.

Scientific metasemiotics, on the other hand, deals with objects which are themselves already scientific signifying systems, such as mathematics, logic, linguistics. Its main concern, therefore, would seem to be a matter of metalanguage.

See also *contract, metalanguage* and *metaterm*.

Metaterm

Any two terms in opposition that constitute a semantic category will also generate a metaterm. Composed of the oppositional relationship of the two original terms, such metaterms, in turn, find their own opposing terms, thereby creating a new semantic category on a hierarchically higher level. Let us take the term *être/*being opposed by the term *paraître/*seeming to be. Both these terms illustrate different sides of the term *truth.* Truth, on the other hand, has its own opposing term in falsehood. Truth and falsehood thus become metaterms with regard to the original terms of *être* and *paraître.*

See also *veridiction.*

Metonymy

The term metonymy designates the procedure whereby a given sentential unit is substituted for another with which it entertains a necessary relationship of contiguity, i.e. cause for effect, container for contained, part for the whole, etc. We may use 'pen' to denote the notion 'author', 'sail' for 'ship', or refer to 'the crown' to indicate the sovereign, the governing power in a monarchy.

See also *metaphor.*

Modal

The term modal is normally used in connection with values or statements. In opposition to descriptive values, modal values are values that contribute to modifying basic statements. Let us take a simple example: 'A monkey sees a banana he wishes to eat. Unfortunately he cannot reach it. So he looks for a stick to help him get the banana within his reach.' In this story the 'stick' which enables the monkey to get the fruit represents a modal value. The banana itself, on the other hand, amounts to a descriptive value.

Similarly, modal statements are used to modify descriptive statements. Thus the sentence 'A monkey wants a banana hanging high in the tree' contains two statements: a descriptive one ('a banana hangs high in the tree') and a modal one ('a monkey wants the banana').

See also *descriptive, modalities, modalization* and *object of value.*

Modalities

The term modalities designates modal expressions such as wanting, having to, ought, may, being able to, knowing how to do. Modalities modify (or overdetermine) basic statements or utterances. These basic statements can be utterances of state or utterances of doing:

(a) utterances of state:
Jack <u>is</u> rich. (basic)
Jack <u>wants to be</u> rich. (modified)

(b) utterances of doing:
Jack <u>killed</u> the dragon. (basic)
Jack <u>had to kill</u> the dragon. (modified)

The modalities can be positive or negative:

Positive: She could swim 50 metres.
Negative: He was unable to do the washing-up.

The basic modalities governing both statements of state or of doing are:

(a) wanting
(1) utterances of state: wanting-to-be (*vouloir être*) – 'He wanted to be rich.'
(2) utterances of doing: wanting-to-do (*vouloir faire*) – 'They want to find the books.'

(b) having to
(1) utterances of state: having-to-be (*devoir être*) – 'She had to be clever.'
(2) utterances of doing: having-to-do (*devoir faire*) – 'He had to do his homework.'

(c) being able
(1) utterances of state: being-able-to-be (*pouvoir être*) – 'She could not have been there.'
(2) utterances of doing: being-able-to-do (*pouvoir faire*) – 'He was able to swim the Channel.'

(d) knowing
(1) utterances of state: knowing-how-to-be (*savoir être*) – 'He knew how to be evil.'
(2) utterances of doing: knowing-how-to-do (*savoir faire*) – 'She knew how to play the piano.'

In the canonical narrative schema of the quest the modalities of wanting-to-do and/or having-to-do are acquired at the stage of the contract. The subject is described as virtual (the virtual subject) and these modalities become the virtualizing modalities. At the qualifying test or stage of competence, the subject acquires in addition the modalities of being-able-to-do and/or knowing-how-to-do. It becomes an actual subject. These modalities therefore are known as the actualizing modalities. The subject is now ready to precede to the next stage, that of the performance.

Further modalities are:

believing: this modal structure governs (or overdetermines) utterances of state – 'She did not believe he would come'.

Mapped out on a semiotic square, the structure of believing would appear as follows:

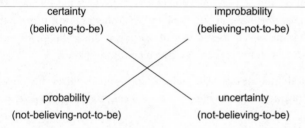

certainty
(believing-to-be)

improbability
(believing-not-to-be)

probability
(not-believing-not-to-be)

uncertainty
(not-believing-to-be)

seeming: here one utterance of state modifies another utterance of state – 'He seems to be an honest person'.

Seeming can be described as a veridictory modality, that is, it relates to the process of truth-telling in a story (veridiction).

See also *alethic modalities, epistemic modalities* and *veridiction.*

Modalization

The term modalization relates to the procedure whereby a descriptive statement is being modified by means of modal expressions. In the event, phrases articulating a wish, mental or physical capacity, a prescription or a direction (wanting, having to, ought, may, being able to, knowing how to, etc.) adjust and ultimately determine the meaning of utterances describing:

(1) a state of being or a state of affairs

Jack <u>is</u> rich.

They <u>are</u> at home.

Jack <u>wants to be</u> rich.

They <u>have to be</u> at home.

Jack <u>might be</u> rich.

They <u>ought to be</u> at home.

(2) an action

Jack <u>killed</u> the dragon.

They <u>build</u> a house

Jack <u>should have killed</u> the dragon.

They <u>are able to build</u> a house.

Jack <u>must have killed</u> the dragon.

They <u>intend to build</u> a house.

See also *modalities.*

Morpheme

A morpheme is the smallest distinctive unit of grammatical analysis and the smallest unit of meaning. Suffixes and prefixes are morphemes. The word 'misogyny' is composed of two morphemes: 'miso' from the Greek *misein,* which means to hate, and 'gyn' from the Greek *gunē,* which means woman. There are two types of morpheme:

1. Lexical morphemes. All prefixes and some suffixes are lexical morphemes used to build new lexical items, e.g. dry-clean-able; anti-static; pre-shrunk.

2. Grammatical morphemes: -ing, or -ed, e.g. ly-ing; dress-ed; miss-ed.

Morphology

In general, the term morphology designates the study of forms, and in particular, those of words. Morphology is thus one of the two fundamental components of grammar, with syntax representing the other. The description of conjugations, verb tenses, adverbs and adjectives or the declension of nouns forms part of morphology, while syntax is concerned with clauses and sentences.

Semiotic theory, when proposing to apply the concept of syntax to elementary structures of signification, introduced also that of morphology. Morphology here relates to taxonomic (classificatory) terms represented on the semiotic square, and syntax to the operations and dynamics they sanction.

The folklorist Vladimir Propp, author of *Morphology of the Folktale*, applies the term not in a linguistic but in a botanical sense, essentially producing a series of 'dramatis personae'.

See also *grammar, Propp* and *syntax*.

Motif

The term motif denotes a distinctive idea or dominant or recurrent theme, feature or pattern in literature, music or the arts. We talk, for example, of the wedding-motif in love stories, of the motif of rags to riches or of the motif of the whore with the heart of gold.

Folklorists such as S. Thompson employ the term *motif* in opposition to *type* of folk-tale in order to designate the smallest story element likely to recur, in its particular form, in popular tradition. Thompson, in fact, is known for his *Motif Index of Folk-Literature*.

Semiotic theory relates the term motif to the concept of configuration because of its particular syntactical and semantic organization as well as its integration into a larger discursive unit.

See also *configuration*.

Myth

The term myth is defined as a symbolic narrative often involving gods or heroes and offering an explanation of some fact or natural phenomenon. Using a different kind of logic, it represents an attempt to impose a graspable shape on human experience and allow for a satisfactory interpretation of human existence. The tale of *Jason and the Argonauts* is a Greek myth and the biblical book of Genesis can be considered a myth with veiled meaning.

Semiotic theory has been influenced by studies of myths from different cultures carried out by Lévi-Strauss. Searching for a semantic structure or 'language system' that underpins culture, he discovered a number of recurrent elements (named 'mythemes') and functions. These seemed to operate like the components of universal signifying structures. Thus Lévi-Strauss found the Oedipus myth to be organized in units set up, like linguistic units, in binary opposition. According to Lévi-Strauss, therefore, it is not the narrative sequence but the structural pattern that gives a myth its meaning.

Myth

In today's culture, the term myth has adopted a wider significance. We talk of bourgeois myths generated by the mass media. In this sense, products or ideas are understood and promoted to confirm and reinforce a particular view of the world and its values. Finally, the term myth is also used simply to indicate a figment of the imagination or a commonly held belief without foundation.

Narrative pivot point

Within the framework of the three tests (qualifying, decisive and glorifying) the narrative pivot point can be considered as the moment of confrontation between a subject and an anti-subject. This confrontation will lead to the domination or victory of one of the protagonists which in turn will determine who possesses the object of value. The narrative pivot point in *Treasure Island* is the battle between Long John Silver and his treacherous crew, who are rivals of the hero in the search for the gold.

The narrative pivot point can only be determined by reading backwards following a line of presupposition. A hierarchy of narrative programmes is thus established.

Narrative programme

The term narrative programme (*programme narratif*, PN) refers to the abstract representation of syntactical relationships and their transformation on the surface level of the utterance.

There are two basic forms of narrative utterances. The first one expresses a *state* of being/possessing: Jack is rich; John has money. This is an *énoncé narratif d'état*. The second type of utterance relates to a doing/action: John works hard; Jack gives money to John. This is an *énoncé narratif de faire*. A narrative programme consists in one utterance relating to action (*énoncé de faire*) affecting two utterances of state (*énoncés d'état*) as a result of transforming a state of being/possessing:

John is poor. Jack gives John money. Now John is rich.

In abstract terms, this is represented in the following way:

$$PN = F\ [S2 \rightarrow (S1 \cap Ov)]$$

F   = function
S1 = John (subject of state)
S2 = Jack (subject of doing)
Ov = money (object of value)
$\cap$ = conjunction with object of value.

In textual analysis, the application of the model of narrative programmes is useful when concentrating on particular aspects of a story. Thus in *Cinderella*, we can analyse the fairy godmother's gifts to the heroine in these terms: the fairy godmother (subject of doing) causes poor Cinderella (subject of state) to be conjoined with an object of value (coach, clothes) which unlike her sisters she does not possess. This narrative sub-programme (PN *d'usage*) can be linked to the basic or macro narrative programme (PN *de base*) of the entire fairy-tale because the fairy godmother's gifts are necessary so that Cinderella (subject of lack) may be conjoined with the objects of wealth, love and happiness at the end of the story.

See also *canonical narrative schema* and *narrative utterance*.

Narrative subject

The term narrative subject designates a particular position in the actantial schema. Other actantial positions are those of object, helper, opponent, sender and receiver.

The narrative subject can be contrasted with the discursive subject and with the epistemological subject or true subject of enunciation.

See also *actantial narrative schema*.

Narrative trajectory

The expression narrative trajectory (or narrative path) describes a movement from one point in a story (quest) to another by way of intermediary stages. In other words, the narrative trajectory of an actant unfolds according to the logical pattern outlined in Greimas's canonical narrative schema. For instance, the stage of competence must always precede that of performance. In Paul Auster's *Moon Palace*, we speak of the narrative trajectory of the actant/subject Marco Fogg which terminates in the finding of his true identity. Before he arrives at his goal, however, he must undergo certain experiences – that of homelessness, for example – which provide him with the necessary competence to achieve his aim successfully.

See also *actant* and *canonical narrative schema*.

Narrative utterance

The term narrative utterance (*énoncé narratif*, EN) is coined to show in abstract terms the relationship/function that exists between two

narrative actants: a subject and an object. There are two basic types of
narrative utterance: a statement relating to a state of being/possessing
and one referring to action.

1. The first one, a narrative utterance of state (*énoncé narratif d'état*)
   indicates a relationship in existence between a subject and an object,
   which at any given moment in the course of a narrative can be
   perceived in terms of being/not being or possessing/not possessing.
   If the relationship is positive, we speak of the subject being
   conjoined with the object. (At the ball Cinderella is conjoined with
   her object/prince.) If, on the other hand, it is negative, the subject is
   disjoined from the object. (Cinderella's absence after the ball
   represents a disjunction.) The abstract representation of a narrative
   utterance of state is as follows:

   EN1 = S$\cap$O (subject conjoined with object)
   EN2 = S$\cup$O (subject disjoined from object)

All narratives are composed of successive transformations of states of
conjunction with objects to those of disjunction and vice versa. These
changes are effected and expressed in the second type of basic narrative
utterance:

2. A statement of doing/action (*énoncé narratif de faire*): the action/
   doing which causes the transformation of state of being/possessing
   does not need to be performed by the subject undergoing the
   change (Cinderella is conjoined with her object/prince as a result of
   her fairy godmother's action: she provides the coach). In the abstract
   formula, therefore, we distinguish S1 (subject of state) from S2
   (subject of doing).

   S2 → (S1$\cap$O)   or   S2→(S1$\cup$O)

The operation itself, that is, one statement of doing affecting and
causing the transformation of two narrative utterances of state, is called
a narrative programme (*programme narratif*, PN).

See also *narrative programme*.

Narratology

The term narratology designates a literary science which generalizes the
linguistic model and applies it to literary texts. Influenced by

structuralism, narratological theory sees the grammatical structure of language reflected in literature: just as we find a sentence composed of a subject and a predicate, so a narrative possesses a syntactical structure recreating this elementary division. The fairy-tale *Cinderella*, for example, is organized, in essence, around a heroine (subject), a doing and a goal (predicate). By pursuing the analogy in greater detail, narratological thought has developed what is now termed a narrative grammar.

The most influential practitioners of narratology have been, apart from Greimas, Tzvetan Todorov, Gérard Genette and Roland Barthes.

See also *structuralism*.

Narrator/narratee

The term narrator denotes an actant in a written text or verbal communication to whom the enunciator – by means of the procedure of *débrayage* – has delegated his/her voice. The 'I' in an utterance, therefore, is not identical with the enunciator but a verbal simulacrum of a narrative presence. Correspondingly, the real enunciatee/receiver of the message is represented in a text by an actant/delegate, the narratee. The latter may, or may not, be present on the discursive level with the mention 'you'.

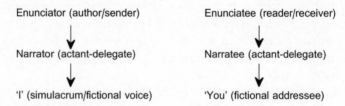

The author Albert Camus is the enunciator of the novel *L'Etranger*. Camus delegates his voice to Meursault, who starts his account with the sentence 'Mother died to-day', and who awaits his execution at the end. Meursault is the narrator, the 'I' in the story, constructed by the enunciator to take his place. The enunciatee of the novel, on the other hand, the reading public, finds its delegate in the construction of a fictional narratee, the implied audience to whom the account is addressed.

See also *enunciator/enunciatee*.

Nature

In opposition to anything artificial or man-made, the term nature designates that which is already given or in a state characteristic of being inborn. In that sense, the concept covers all natural phenomena from plants, animals, landscapes, etc. to the inherent and innate characteristics of human beings.

In semiotic theory, the notion of nature is seen as coexisting and contrasting with that of **culture**. Thus in the description of a seaside town, expressions such as 'coast', 'waves', 'wind' or 'sea' belong to the semantic category *nature* while references to 'houses', 'road', 'cars' and 'boats' relate to that of *culture*. Equally, in a murder story, mention of premeditation and planning the evil deed fall in the category of cultural behaviour while the rendering of the actual killing with its gory details would be classed under violence of natural origin.

Following Lévi-Strauss, semiotics considers the opposing couple nature/culture to articulate the semantic category 'social life' whereas the semantic category 'life/death' characterizes the universe of the individual.

See also *culture*.

Negative

The two terms of the axis of contraries, S1 and S2, are labelled respectively the **positive** and the negative term. These terms do not imply any thymic connotation (i.e. euphoric or dysphoric). In the category freedom/imprisonment, for instance, freedom is the positive term and imprisonment the negative term:

S1 ———————————	S2
freedom	imprisonment
positive	negative

However, depending on the context, both terms could have euphoric or dysphoric connotations. The escaped prisoner, for example, feels unhappy about imprisonment (dysphoria) while a starving tramp might be glad to be locked up (euphoria).

See also *positive, semiotic square* and *thymic*.

Nominalization

In Halliday's terminology, nominalization is a structural feature whereby any element or group of elements in a clause is made to function as a nominal group (as a noun). Any nominalization, therefore, constitutes a single element in the message structure: 'What the man did with the violin (= nominal group) was to give it to his friend'; 'The one I like best (= nominal group) is not in the shop.'

Nominalizations are frequently formed from verbs. They express, therefore, a process: 'Stealing from people will not get you anywhere'; 'The building of the department store took six months'; 'The killing took place in the morning'.

Critical linguistics has drawn attention to the ideological weight carried by nominalizations, especially in the field of media discourse. Norman Fairclough, for example, has pointed out that the conversion of verbs to nouns in particular is a means of rendering a discourse more abstract, thereby enhancing its 'truth effect'. The omission of agency also allows one to background (or even ignore) historical detail.

Object of value

The term value has itself several meanings. We differentiate, for example, between value understood through 'valuation', or estimated worth or price, and value understood as 'quality' which makes someone or something worthy of esteem, desirable or important.

Semiotic theory describes value as arising from the relationship between actantial subjects and objects: any subject's need or desire for a particular object makes the latter valuable, turning it into an *objet de valeur* in the process. Moreover, the value it has for the subject comes to be identified with the object. For instance, if someone buys a car, it is probably not so much a question of owning the object/car but rather of acquiring an easy and comfortable means of transport, or a way of enhancing one's social reputation, or enjoying a feeling of power … The thing itself, in this case, is merely pretext, a placement for the desired values. Thus, in semiotic analysis, the term object of value has been fashioned to designate objects placed in relation to subjects.

Onomatopoeia

The term onomatopoeia refers to the process whereby a word is formed in imitation of the sound produced by the thing meant. The word 'bang', for instance, sounds like the sudden loud noise to which it is referring. The 's' at the beginning of the words 'snake' or 'serpents' likewise conveys the hissing sound made by these animals. Onomatopoeia is a figure of speech that is often found in poetry, sometimes in prose. 'Myriads of rivulets hurrying thro' the lawn, / The moan of doves in immemorial elms, / And murmuring of innumerable bees' (Tennyson).

Opponent

Any actant who hinders the subject in its quest is known as an opponent. Unlike the anti-subject, the opponent does not have a quest of its own. In an athlete's attempts to acquire a gold medal at the Olympics, for example, physical fatigue and age may act as opponents.

See also *anti-subject*.

P

Paradigm

The term paradigm refers to a group of sentential units susceptible to occupy the same place, or replace each other, in a syntagmatic chain. In other words, paradigmatic elements exist on the vertical axis of language and could be substituted for one another in the same set. The relationship they entertain is one of equivalence or opposition. Thus 'building', 'house', 'hovel' or 'palace' may be substituted for 'dwelling'; on the other hand, 'out' could be replaced by its opposition 'in' in the sentence 'she stayed in' instead of 'she stayed out'.

See also *syntagm*.

Paraphrase

A paraphrase is a restatement of the text's meaning in different words, i.e. it is a discursive unit that is semantically equivalent to another unit previously produced. Paraphrases are often introduced with 'what I mean to say', 'in other words', 'i.e.', etc.

The operation is one of translation (of meaning) and of expansion.

Paratopic

Paratopic space is the space in which the qualifying test takes place, that is, in which competence is acquired. It is contrasted with utopic space, where the decisive test takes place and the performances are carried out.

In *Treasure Island*, the sea voyage with its encounters with pirates constitutes the paratopic space of the qualifying test. In *Cinderella*, the house where she acquires a new dress, as well as the journey in the coach to the ball, can be considered paratopic spaces.

See also *topic space*.

Passion

In semiotic terms, passion is perceived as syntagmatic organization of 'psychic states' or 'states of the mind' (*états d'âme*). Thus it belongs to the category of states of being (*être*) as opposed to action/doing (*faire*). Such passionate conditions/states are analysable on the textual surface of an utterance. They are often expressed in figurative simulacra underpinning a narrative action. The sudden discovery of love may be evoked in a storm, a flash of lightning; or greed depicted in excessive eating.

Passion is always linked to a subject either having completed an action or being in the process of performing an action. Othello kills Desdemona in a fit of jealousy. He is torn by remorseful passion after her death.

See also *emotion* and *semiotics of passion*.

Pathematic role

The term pathematic comes from the Greek and relates to passions or emotions. Thus in contrast to a thematic role which is linked to doing/action (*faire*) a pathematic role relates to a subject's state of being (*être*), namely that characterized by emotion. An actor possessing a pathematic role is often described by reference to a stereotyped passion which renders emotionally geared behaviour predictable. In Dickens's *A Christmas Carol*, for instance, Scrooge has the thematic role of a businessman and the pathematic role of a miser.

In general terms, pathematic roles can be grouped under the overall heading of actors' thematic description on the surface level of an utterance, thereby contributing to actorial individualization. In most instances, socially defined themes or functions outweigh in importance the pathematic input. There are exceptions, however, such as Scrooge, whose stereotyping as a miser overrides his social description.

See also *emotion* and *semiotics of passion*.

Patient

The term patient designates the narrative role of a subject of state, that is of a subject whose relationship with an object remains unchanged. This kind of relationship is frequently expressed in verbs such as 'to be' or 'to have'. In the sentence 'John has blue eyes', 'John' is a subject of state or a 'patient', just as 'Brian' would be in the sentence 'Brian is poor'.

The term patient also designates the narrative role of a subject whose transformation of state in a narrative programme is the result of the action of another subject. In the sentence 'Paul was given a book by his friend', 'Paul' takes the role of a 'patient'.

The term patient contrasts with the term agent, which refers to the narrative role of a subject of doing, that is, of a subject engaged in the carrying out of a particular narrative programme.

See also *agent, subject of doing* and *subject of state.*

Performance

The term performance designates the principal action of the subject, the event to which the story has been leading. It is by carrying out the performance that the subject acquires (or fails to acquire) the object of value. This stage of the canonical narrative schema is also known as the decisive test.

Performance always presupposes competence, doing implies a wanting-to-do as well as an ability-to-do (being able to and/or knowing how to). Sitting an examination (performance) implies the acquisition of a number of skills as well as an initial desire/obligation to succeed (competence).

See also *canonical narrative schema.*

Performative

In Austin's terminology, a performative utterance not only describes the action of the speaker but also performs the same action.

Examples: 'I promise to be there at three o'clock'; 'The chairman declared the meeting open'. In both cases, the utterance embodies the act to which it refers: that of promising or of opening the meeting. Performative utterances, therefore, can be contrasted with those utterances that simply describe an action.

The term performative would seem to be synonymous with illocutionary, a term indicating speech acts that involve commands, questions, warnings, etc.

See also *illocutionary act* and *perlocutionary act.*

Perlocutionary act

The term perlocutionary act is used in the speech act theory (Austin) to describe an utterance that brings about an effect upon the actions, feelings or thoughts of the listener. A political speech, for instance, represents a perlocutionary act in that it produces an effect on its audience that may be one of enthusiasm, conviction or indifference.

A perlocutionary act can be contrasted with an illocutionary act, an utterance that accomplishes something in the act of speaking, such as performing the act of promising by saying 'I promise'. The notion of perlocution belongs partly to cognitive semiotics and partly to the semiotics of emotion.

See also *illocutionary act*.

Personification

Personification refers to a narrative process whereby an object (a thing, abstract or non-human being) is attributed qualities which allow it to be considered as a subject. It is therefore endowed with a narrative programme and capable of performing a doing. To give an example: 'The city opened its mouth and slowly devoured the inhabitants within its entrails.'

Persuasive doing

Persuasive doing describes the cognitive act whereby an enunciator manipulates an enunciatee, persuading the latter to believe something (*faire croire*) or to act in a certain way (*faire faire*). If someone suggests to me that I might like to enter a fishing contest, that person is exerting a persuasive doing (*faire faire*). If a politician tries to persuade us (*faire croire*) that stringent measures need to be taken to get the economy working, our acceptance of his proposition shows his persuasive doing to have been effective.

Phatic function

If a communication focuses on the contact between addresser (sender) and addressee (receiver), then the phatic function dominates. In general, the phatic function relies on utterances that do not elicit or offer information but simply establish contact (e.g. 'Good morning'), maintain it (e.g. 'How are you?'), or break it (e.g. 'Goodbye'). Most conversation about the weather has this function.

Dominance of the phatic function in a text does not preclude the other speech functions from being present to varying degrees.

See also *communication model.*

Phoneme

A phoneme is a minimal unit of potentially meaningful sound within a language's system of recognized sound distinctions. It is, for example, the phonemic distinction in English between /l/ and /r/ which enables us to recognize the difference between the words 'level' and 'revel' or 'room' and 'loom'.

For Saussure the linguistic signifier can be described as a collection of sounds or a chain of phonemes, whereas the signified corresponds to the concept or idea conveyed by these sounds.

See also *signifier and signified.*

Phonemics

Phonemics is the branch of linguistics that analyses the sound system of languages.

See also *phonetics.*

Phonetics

Phonetics is the study of the physical sounds of human speech. It includes the production, transmission and perception of sounds. Phonetics can be contrasted with phonology, which is concerned not only with sounds but more importantly with the relationship between sounds and meaning.

Poetic or aesthetic function

When a communication focuses on its message for its own sake, then the poetic or aesthetic function can be said to be dominant. In other words, the poetic function foregrounds the way a message is expressed rather than concentrating on what is said and the 'reality beyond'.

Attention may be drawn, for example, to sound patterns, diction and syntax. In poetry, the poetic function is usually dominant.

Dominance of the poetic function in a communication does not exclude the other speech functions being present to varying degrees.

See also *communication model*.

Polysemy

The term polysemy designates the presence of more than one sememe (meaning) within a lexeme (word). The word 'head' is polysemic, as it would appear in the dictionary as (a) a part of the body or (b) a leader, as in the expression 'Head of State'.

Polysemic lexemes can be contrasted with monosemic lexemes, which involve only a single sememe. These are characteristic of specialized discourses: the word 'Internet', for example, is monosemic.

Positive

The two terms of the axis of contraries, S1 and S2, are called respectively positive and **negative** even though these qualifications do not involve a thymic connotation (euphoric or dysphoric).

In the category life/death, life is the positive term and death the negative:

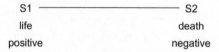

S1	S2
life	death
positive	negative

This is equally true of stories where death may be the object of desire (e.g. accounts of martyrdom).

See also *negative, semiotic square* and *thymic*.

Pragmatic

Contrary to the meaning allotted to pragmatic in the English language, semiotic theory uses the term with the meaning given to it in French, that is, as relating to action, to practical doing. Accordingly, the two fundamental dimensions of narrative are termed one pragmatic and the other cognitive. The pragmatic dimension refers to external, physical events such as killing a giant, catching a thief or digging a flower bed. The cognitive dimension, on the other hand, relates to internal mental activities such as knowing, convincing, deceiving, etc. The importance attached to each dimension varies according to the nature of the discourse. In adventure stories, *Treasure Island* for example, it is the pragmatic dimension that dominates, whereas in legal discourse it is the cognitive.

In recent years attention has been focused on a third dimension of narrative known as the thymic dimension. This relates to feelings of euphoria or dysphoria (i.e. pleasant or unpleasant) experienced by the actors. These feelings can be correlated with the stages of a narrative programme. They can, for example, describe a state of disjunction or conjunction with an object of value. In *Romeo and Juliet*, Juliet's disjunction from Romeo, the object of her desire, takes shape in her despair giving rise to her suicide.

See also *cognitive* and *thymic*.

Process

Along the lines of the Saussurian division of language into *langue* and *parole*, Hjelmslev separates the general practice of giving meaning to objects into a process (*parole*) and a **system** (*langue*). Process here represents the syntagmatic axis of language and system the paradigmatic axis from which signs are chosen.

In semiotic theory, the term process designates narrative doing which is lexicalized either in the form of a simple verb or enlarged in a sentence, a paragraph or a chapter. 'Running', 'singing' or 'cooking' thus describe a process just as does the full statement 'The cook took flour, eggs, milk and butter and produced a delicious cake.'

A semiotic process always comprises three stages: the inchoative, durative and terminative stages. A strike, for example, analysed as a process has an inchoative stage (tools are put down), a duration (the gates remain closed) and a terminative stage (a solution is found and work restarts).

See also *language* and *system*.

A Russian formalist who developed the notion of narrative grammar, V. I. Propp exerted a strong influence on structuralism and on semiotics. An examination of numerous folk-tales led Propp to conclude that there exist thirty-one functions which are common to them all. Functions represent units of narrative such as 'a difficult task is proposed to the hero', or 'the villain is punished'. The functions are distributed amongst seven 'spheres of action'. These are:

(1) villain
(2) donor (provider)
(3) helper
(4) the princess (a sought-for person) and her father
(5) the dispatcher
(6) the hero
(7) the false hero

These 'spheres of action' were later simplified by Greimas to produce his own actantial schema.

See also *actantial narrative schema, donor, helper, traitor* and *villain*.

Qualification

Qualification designates the process whereby a subject becomes fully competent, i.e. s/he must be in possession of the modalities of being-able-to-do and/or knowing-how-to-do acquired at the stage of the qualifying test. The process of qualification can be contrasted with those of the establishment of the subject (the contract), the realization of the subject (the decisive test or performance) and the sanction of the subject (the glorifying test).

See also *canonical narrative schema, modalities* and *qualifying test.*

Qualifying test

This is the stage in the canonical narrative schema at which competence is acquired. By competence is meant the qualities that make it possible to carry out an action successfully. These qualities are known as the modalities. They are in the first instance:

(a) a wanting-to-do (*vouloir faire*) and/or (b) a having-to-do (*devoir faire*)

In order to perform an action, the subject must initially desire to act, or feel under an obligation to act. These modalities are usually acquired at the opening stage of the contract/manipulation: they are subsequently manifested (and sometimes challenged) in the qualifying test. James Bond, for example, has been ordered to steal some secret plans (the contract). Embarking on this quest and planning the theft are a manifestation of his desire and represent part of the qualifying test.

The desire or obligation to act, however, is not in itself sufficient. The subject also needs to acquire a further qualification at this stage: it must be in possession of at least one of the following modalities:

(a) a being-able-to-do (*pouvoir faire*): If your object is to break into some premises (decisive test), then you must possess the necessary ability, that is, a key or some other means of entry. This will then become your helper. And/or you must possess:

(b) a knowing-how-to-do (*savoir faire*): Any means of illegal entry is of little value to you if you do not know how to use it. If you are sitting a French examination (decisive test) it is assumed that you have acquired the skills associated with learning French (the qualifying test). If your goal is to find the hidden treasure on a desert island, the qualifying test could take the form of a sea voyage. It could also be represented in episodes where maps of the hidden treasure are acquired. If the subject fails in the qualifying test (e.g., the ship sinks), then the quest is terminated. In *Cinderella*, the fairy godmother functions as helper to provide the young girl with the necessary competence (clothes, coach) enabling her to fulfil her dreams and go to the ball (decisive test).

See also *canonical narrative schema*.

Quest

The quest is a figurative term designating the movement (or displacement) of a subject towards the desired object of value. In general terms, this movement is always from a relationship of disjunction with the object of value towards one of conjunction with it. For instance, Jason's quest for the Golden Fleece begins the moment he leaves home and sets sail for Colchis. It is completed when he is successfully conjoined with his object of value, the Golden Fleece.

For a quest to be successful, a series of logical stages must be completed. These are presented and explained in Greimas's canonical narrative schema.

See also *canonical narrative schema*.

R

Reader

The term reader describes the receiver of a message or discourse. We speak of a reader of a written text, of sign language or any sign system (colour, dance, music, etc.) that requires decoding to be understood.

In semiotics the term enunciatee is used in preference to reader.

See also *enunciator/enunciatee*.

Reality

In semiotic theory, the term reality always refers to constructed reality. In everyday life, this relates to the signification with which we invest the world that surrounds us. The *reality effect*, then, corresponds to the relationship between that world and the subject (i.e. us) which is activated by some kind of *embrayage* or engagement, that is, by making our presence felt in the constructed environment.

There are two processes that help setting up reality effects in discourse. The first one is iconization. This relates to the procedure whereby an impression of the referential world outside the text is produced and sustained. The topographical description in Zola's *Germinal*, for instance, creates an illusion of reality.

Figurativization of discourse represents another, though related, way of constructing effects of being real. All elements in a text that refer to the external physical world and can be apprehended by the five senses belong to the figurative level. They are essential ingredients in the creation of an illusion of reality. A journalist seeking to present an event as vividly as possible, for example, might evoke sounds, colours or smells in his description to produce an impression of immediacy and realism.

See also *embrayage, figurativization* and *iconicity*.

Realization

The term realization is used in narrative semiotics when describing modes of junction between a subject and an object. Before any kind of conjunction or disjunction takes place, subjects and objects are placed in a position of virtuality. When they are in a position of disjunction, we talk of actualization. Realization refers to the transformation which reverses an earlier disjunction to bring about a conjunction between a subject and an object. Wishing to possess a car, for instance, and having enough money to purchase the desired object but not having done so yet describes a situation of actualization. However, once the purchase has taken place, the object (car) is conjoined with the desiring subject, reversing the earlier situation of disjunction. This transformation is called a realization.

See also *actualization* and *virtualization*.

Receiver

The receiver represents the actant to whom a desire or obligation is given by a sender. This process or transaction must take place before the receiver can embark on a quest, i.e. before the receiver can assume the function of a subject. In the Falklands War, the soldier/receiver became the subject of a quest only when he had decided to accept his mission or contract to go and fight.

See also *sender.*

Reference

In Halliday's terminology, reference describes the process whereby one element introduced at one place in a text can be taken as a reference point for something that follows. Reference words (or referring expressions) are words which possess only partial meaning: to work out their full significance on any particular occasion we have to refer to something else. Examples of reference words are pronouns and deictics. To give an example: 'I lived in Paris for several years. I was very happy there.' The deictic 'there', in this case, has only limited meaning unless one reads it as referring back to a particular location, i.e. 'Paris'.

See also *cohesion* and *referential cohesion.*

Referent

The referent is the entity to which a word refers or which it stands for in the outside world, or in extra-linguistic reality. The referent can be an object, a quality, actions or real events. The referent of the word 'cow' is the animal, cow.

The referent can also involve the imaginary world, as is the case with the word 'chimera'. Or it can stand for a description, or an idea, expressed in a whole complex of words. The referent of A. J. Ayer's *Language, Truth and Logic* is the philosophical theory of verifiablility.

Referential cohesion

In Halliday's theory of discourse, referential cohesion is a type of textual cohesion that is produced by the process of reference. It is characterized by the presence of what is known as reference words (or referring expressions). Reference words are words which do not give their full meaning to the objects of the world (the referent): to work out what they mean on any one particular occasion, we need to refer to something else. There are three categories of reference words:

(a) *personal* reference words or pronouns: 'The girls arrived late at school because they had missed the bus.'

(b) *demonstrative* reference words or demonstratives: 'He bought me the book that I really wanted.'

(c) *comparative* reference words or a reference that is based on contrast: 'I like this dress better than that.'

See also *cohesion.*

Referential function

If a communication is orientated towards the context or world (real or imaginary) outside the text, then it is the referential function that dominates. A good example are texts whose principal aim is to convey information, such as car manuals or recipe books. In literature, it is often when an illusion of the real world is being constructed that the referential function can be said to be dominant. 'The house stood in the best part of town. It had two storeys, five bedrooms and a very big garden that was more like a park' is an example of the referential function dominating.

Dominance of the referential function in a communication does not exclude the other speech functions, which will also be present to varying degrees.

See also *communication model.*

Reiteration

Reiteration designates a form of lexical cohesion in which two cohesive items refer to the same entity or event. Reiterative devices include: repetition, the use of synonyms or near-synonyms, of subordinates and generals.

In the following example, the underlined words refer to the same entity: 'She is having terrible trouble with her car. The thing won't start in the morning.'

See also *cohesion*.

Renunciation

The term renunciation characterizes the position of a subject of state when it deprives itself of an object of value. The act is one of reflexive disjunction. For example, 'Mary gives away all her money'. The abstract representation of this relationship is as follows:

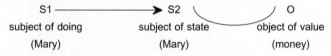

S1	→	S2		O
subject of doing		subject of state		object of value
(Mary)		(Mary)		(money)

See also *appropriation* and *attribution*.

Repeated event

A repeated event is an event which occurs once and is narrated more than once. An example would be the murder of Hammond in W. Somerset Maugham's short story *The Letter*. A repeated event can be compared to events that are singular or iterative.

See also *iterative* and *singular*.

Rhetoric

The term rhetoric designates the theory and practice of eloquence, the artful use of language as a means of persuasion. Originally associated with the classics, the art of rhetoric is still alive today. One example is court proceedings, where both prosecution and defence are trying not only with facts but also with words and speeches to convince the jury of the justice of their cause.

Rhetoric In a semiotic perspective, rhetoric is considered a pre-scientific theory of discourse whose organization resembles that of semiotics. Its fundamental three-part structure, however, of *dispositio* (discursive segmentation), *inventio* (discursive themes) and *elocutio* (syntactic and verbal figures and configurations) is applied to persuasive discourse only.

See also *persuasive doing.*

Sanction

The term sanction designates the stage of the quest where the subject's principal action or performance is being evaluated/interpreted by the narrator or an actor in the story. For instance, the performance could be considered a success or a failure, the subject could be rewarded or punished. It is at this stage that the subject undergoes the glorifying test.

See also *canonical narrative schema*.

Secret

On the semiotic square of veridiction, the term secret subsumes the complementary terms of being and non-seeming which are located on the positive pole or deixis.

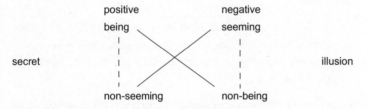

See also *deixis* and *veridiction*.

Seeming

Seeming constitues one pole of the semantic category 'truth' which combines seeming (*paraître*) and being (*être*). The terms of being and seeming are therefore in a relationship of opposition while also expressing the two faces – or each asserting one aspect – of truth.

See also *veridiction*.

Semantic category

A semantic category is formed by two terms in opposition while possessing at least one common denominator. In other words, they are contraries linked by presupposition in the way that 'in' presupposes 'out' or 'good' presupposes 'evil'. The semantic category itself comprises the two opposing poles in one umbrella term which illustrates their common feature: 'in' and 'out', for example, belong to the semantic category of 'space'; the semantic category of 'temperature' comprises the two poles 'hot' versus 'cold', that of 'verticality' the opposing poles 'up' and 'down'.

Semantic field

A semantic field comprises all the meanings (semes) attached to a particular signifier in the text. The signifier 'fame' may thus include the meaning 'celebrity', 'stardom', 'repute', 'honour', 'glory' or 'eminence', 'illustriousness'; the semantic field of 'joke' might comprise 'witticism' and 'anecdote' or 'prank', 'trick', etc.

The term semantic field is often interchangeable with that of lexical field.

See also *lexical field*.

Semantics

The term semantics designates a branch of linguistics which deals with the meaning given to words or syntagms. In other words, semantics concerns itself with a scientific description of the level of the signified in language rather than the signifier.

In the context of semiotic grammar, semantics represents one of its main components, with syntax making up the other. Semantics, here, relates to the three levels of meaning. Firstly, there is abstract or *conceptual semantics*, which is concerned with meaning at the deep level, the *ab quo* where signification starts. An example are elementary abstract concepts underlying a text such as 'war' and 'peace', or 'virtue' and 'sin', in other words, terms in opposition forming semantic categories. Their organization and dynamics within a text, however, fall under the heading of syntax.

Secondly, there is *narrative semantics*, actualizing values on the story level, selecting them and placing them in conjunction or disjunction with subjects, that is, setting up states of being ready to be transformed. The fairy-tale *Cinderella*, for example, selects happiness and riches as values to aim for, and places these initially in disjunction with the heroine and in conjunction with the nasty sisters. The ensuing narrative programme, on the other hand, the actual process of transformation, in Cinderella's case the achievement of wealth and happiness, is subject to narrative syntax.

Finally, *discursive semantics* puts values into words by giving them figurative and thematic shape. It is here that we encounter reality effects such as references to the senses (vision, touch, etc.) as well as allusion to concrete or abstract worlds. Using *Cinderella* again as an example, we find wealth expressed in lavish clothes and sumptuous balls, and happiness taking the shape of the love of a handsome prince. The syntagmatic organization of these discursive elements belongs to discursive syntax.

See also *grammar* and *syntax.*

Seme

A seme is the smallest common denominator within a unit of meaning. In the sentence 'The summer sun burnt our skin', 'heat' would be the predominant seme; the film title *Trains, Planes and Automobiles* illustrates the seme 'travel'.

See also *lexeme* and *sememe.*

Sememe

A sememe is the totality of semes that are actualized by a term within a given context. In Blake's poetry the following sememe could be attached to the term 'city': industrial, black, crowded, poverty, pain, evil, filth, noise.

See also *lexeme.*

Semic density

The expression semic density relates to the greater or lesser number of semes that enter the composition of a sememe. The greater the number of themes actualized by a term within a given context, the greater is its semic density. Stanza 2 of Tennyson's 'The Charge of the Light Brigade' offers an example of high semic density: 'Some one had blunder'd: / Their's not to make reply, / Their's not to reason why, / Their's but to do and die.' These four lines evoke the semes of error, unreason, proscription and death in connection with the main seme of obedience.

See also *seme* and *sememe.*

Semiology

In contrast to semiotics, which is concerned with the theory and analysis of the production of meaning, semiology refers to the study of sign systems in operation such as codes, including those of linguistic signs. Explicit meanings resulting from the conjunction of a signifier and a signified are investigated. The traffic code is a case in point: to those familiar with the conventions, 'red' means 'stop' and 'green' means 'go'. Nonetheless, there are cases when semiology and semiotics overlap.

The term semiology was coined by Saussure to cover the theory of sign systems, and for a long time was used alongside semiotics with very little difference in meaning. Today the Greimassian School distinguishes clearly between the study of sign *systems* (semiology) and the study of the *process* of the generation of meaning (semiotics).

See also *semiotics*.

Semiotic square

According to Saussure 'il n'y a de sens que dans la différence' and according to Hjelmslev language is fundamentally a system of relationships rather than signs. Thus, in the analysis of meaning, semiotics proceeds from the recognition of differences to the definition of the relationships underpinning them. In the event, the semiotic square is no more than a visual representation of the elementary structure of meaning. It is the logical expression of any semantic category. This elementary structure is defined by three relationships:

1. *Opposition or contrariety*. Meaning is viewed essentially as a product of opposition: there can be no 'up' without 'down', no 'good' without 'evil'. In order to be in opposition or in a relationship of contrariety, two terms (frequently referred to as S1 and S2) must have a feature in common, e.g. 'hot' and 'cold' have the notion of temperature in common: temperature here is known as the complex term. 'High' and 'low' have the notion of verticality in common, their complex term is verticality. S1, therefore, presupposes the existence of S2.

2. *Contradiction.* In order to move from S1 to S2 you must first of all negate S1 (written −S1). If you want to go from 'high' to 'low', for instance, you must move via 'non-high'. 'Non-high' (−S1), then, becomes the contradictory term. If S1 is 'good', then −S1 is 'non-good'. If S2 is 'evil', −S2 is 'non-evil'.

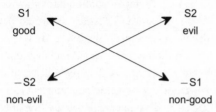

3. The third relationship which seals the square is one of *implication or complementarity*. This is built on the connection between a term and the negation of its opposite: 'good' implies 'non-evil', 'high' implies 'non-low'. It is equivalent to the act of assertion, demonstrating the coherence of meaning. For if 'good' does not imply 'non-evil', then our original pair 'good/evil' with their contradictories belong to different semantic categories. S1 and −S2 or S2 and −S1 are therefore defined as complementary terms.

The semiotic square can be used as a tool in the analysis not only of individual semantic concepts but also of longer units of meaning such as paragraphs or whole texts. In this case fundamental semantic oppositions underpinning the unit have to be extracted and placed in the positions of S1 and S2.

Semiotics

Semiotics is the theory of signification, that is, of the generation or production of meaning. In contrast to semiology, which studies sign systems and their organization (e.g. traffic codes, sign language), semiotics concerns itself with *how* meaning is produced. In other words, what interests the semiotician is what makes an utterance meaningful, how it signifies and what precedes it on a deeper level to result in the manifestation of meaning.

Semiotic theory is based on the belief that meaning is not inherent in objects, that they do not signify by themselves, but that meaning is *constructed* by a competent observer – a subject – capable of giving 'form' to objects. To give an example: confronted with an implement from a different culture, say African or Asian, we would probably be incapable of immediately grasping its significance. However, left alone with it, we will give it a meaning that is based on what knowledge we have and what will suit our purposes. The semiotician thus sees the whole of our signifying universe – including statements about it – as the product of a presupposed semiotic competence, the only one able to construct its signification.

The semiotic working method derives from the assumption that the structures underlying – and resulting in – the production of meaning are susceptible to hypothetical representation in the shape of models. The justness of particular models is confirmed or invalidated through testing them against the semiotic object – such as a text – to which they are meant to be applicable. Semiotic analysis by students of literature makes use of such models to decode effects of meaning perceptible on the surface of a text.

See also *semiology*.

Semiotics of passion

At first glance, passion, linked to ethics and conditions of the mind, would seem to belong to the realms of classical philosophy, psychology or sociology rather than semiotics. What rules could there be that passion obeys, what models to describe passionate behaviour or its simulacra?

Semiotics has from the very beginning recognized and incorporated into its theory the contribution made by affective (thymic) states to the production of meaning. Thus it has been accepted that positive or negative assessment of values depends also on a subject's euphoric or dysphoric frame of mind. This is borne out by statements such as 'I know that you are right but I don't believe you'; it is also evident in the appreciation of an object – a car, a novel – whose acceptance or rejection is usually based on a combination of practical/rational and emotional/aesthetic considerations.

When it comes to passion, however, that is, strong feeling or agitation of the mind, semiotic analysis on the narrative and discursive levels of an utterance is more complex. Being related to states of mind/ conditions of the soul (*états d'âme*) rather than action/doing (*faire*), passion does not obey the pattern of the actantial and canonical schemas of the narrative quest. Yet passion does play an important part because it will affect the subject's doing in one of two ways: either impassioned feelings will dominate the action (*dominance pathémique*) or passion will be present yet on the surface be dominated by the cognitive or actional dimensions (*dominance cognitive*) of the narrative. Either way it is analysable on the structural and organizational level of the discourse.

1. Passion dominating action/doing (*faire*) is illustrated by the *crime passionnel*. A discursive utterance governed by passion is marked by:

   – an unstable relationship between the narrative subject and object. Apart from its position of object the latter may also adopt those of sender or manipulator (e.g. 'Love' motivates the subject or makes it do something); or even of subject of doing (the object of a passion moves, disturbs, thereby acting on, even transforming, the subject that becomes 'moved'). Thus the subject itself may also take on the function of object (e.g. become a 'victim' of jealousy). Finally, the subject is often affected in its very core by the object of its passion and behaves in an abnormal way (a gentle person having fits of rage or even murdering). Thus we have a subject and an object with altered and changing modal capacities.

   – the importance attached to *absence*: the unstable relationship is accompanied by a proliferation of images focusing on the desired object and dwelling on the absence which it reveals but which also reveals it. 'La sensibilité est une émotion de l'absence' (Bertrand, 1988). 'How like a winter hath my absence been / From thee, the pleasure of the fleeting year! / What freezings have I felt, what dark days seen! / What old December's bareness every where!' (Shakespeare, Sonnet 97).

Most love poetry could serve as an example, as indeed most literature concerned with passion.

— aspectual indications: deep emotion, strong passion are usually characterized by the suddenness of their discovery. One moment the subject does not understand what is happening, the next awareness strikes and all is clear. The very suddenness of the revelation thus becomes a hallmark of the emotion as well as of its strength.

2. Passion dominated by practical or cognitive action is illustrated by subjects giving in to reason/advice in preference to passion. The dutiful daughter complying with her parents' wishes not to marry her unsuitable lover would be a case in point. A discursive utterance in which passion is governed by the cognitive dimension is marked by:

— a stabilization of the object, which becomes, as it were, 'objective'. The object is held at a distance, considered objectively and analysed. Thus after a major accident or a personal tragedy provoking strong emotions, people tend to go over what happened again and again, examining every detail as though the exact re-structuring of the event were all-important.

— an epistemic subject concerned with accurate knowledge and the establishment of truth. It is given over totally to a descriptive and analytical competence. In *La Prisonnière*, for instance, Proust's narrator scrutinizes and takes apart one insignificant remark made by the heroine Albertine, endlessly searching it and hypothesizing about its precise meaning. The underlying motive for this cognitive investigation is, of course, of a passionate nature, in this case: jealousy.

— a concern for veridiction is at stake. It matters to establish the truth once and for all, thereby trying to dominate emotional uncertainty. It is important to discover a truth that the subject can believe. But this truth, says Stendhal, 'n'est en vérité qu'un soupir'.

Finally, it should be noted that passion does not only find expression in verbal discourse. Passion can also be manifest in, for example, spatial, visual or musical utterances.

See also *aspectualization, passion, pathematic role* and *thymic.*

The term semi-symbolic designates a particular relationship between expression and content, or signifier and signified. Nodding one's head to signify 'yes', would be an example, or shaking it to mean 'no'.

The term semi-symbolic is applied in particular to the visual arts, where movement, gesture, colour, etc., acquire specific values. In a particular picture, for instance, light colours and simplicity of outline may be associated with happiness, whereas their opposite – dark colours and blurred lines – may be associated with unhappiness.

The concept semi-symbolic differs from symbolic in that the relationship between signifier and signified relates to categories rather than units. Nodding yes or no, for example, uses the vertical axis to affirm and the horizontal to deny, thus linking the category of spatial axes to that of assertion versus negation. Or a semi-symbolic representation of the category good versus evil may be found in nature where a mountain is associated with God and an abyss with the devil. In the case of a symbol, on the other hand, the relationship between expression and content is one of two individual units: a set of scales symbolizes justice; a rose symbolizes love.

See also *semantic category* and *symbol*.

Sender

The term sender normally belongs to the narrative level of an utterance, where it represents the actantial instance (person or idea) that motivates an action or causes something to happen. The sender not only institutes the values to aim for but also transmits the desire or obligation to pursue them to a subject. Any quest begins with an initial contract between a sender and a receiver/subject accepting the mandate, and ends with a sender's (not necessarily the same as the mandating sender) sanction, that is, an evaluation of the subject's performance.

In their quest to defeat the Argentinians, the soldiers who took part in the Falklands War had two senders: (a) an external sender in the figures of Mrs Thatcher and the rest of the British Government, and (b) an internal sender in the belief in patriotism and in the traditional ideology of warfare.

See also *receiver*.

Sender-adjudicator

The sender normally occupies the positions of mandatory sender and of sender-adjudicator.

At the beginning of a narrative programme, the sender establishes a contract with the future subject and instigates the system of values in accordance with which the subject must act. The sender here is sometimes referred to as the mandatory sender to distinguish it from the later role of sender-adjudicator. The latter is the sender who intervenes at the stage of sanction or the glorifying test. At this point the performance of the subject is being judged with regard to the original mandate. In a fairy-tale, the king (as mandatory sender) asks the knight to slay the dragon. At the end of the story he judges (as sender-adjudicator) the deed to have been accomplished to his satisfaction by giving him his daughter in marriage.

The roles of mandatory sender and of sender-adjudicator, however, are not always held by the same actor. In a military conflict, the defeated army is usually judged not by their mandating government (mandatory sender) but by their victorious enemy (sender-adjudicator). Students in higher education are often awarded degrees not by their teachers (mandatory sender) but by State examiners (sender-adjudicator).

Shifter

Introduced by Jakobson, the term shifter is equivalent in meaning to the semiotic terms engager or disengager. A *disengager* is a word that shifts the discourse away from the point of enunciation by setting up an action, a time and a place different from those of the person who is speaking. For instance, 'at that time' (as opposed to the moment of speaking) 'he' (as opposed to the speaker) 'was living in Paris' (as opposed to the place of enunciation).

An *engager*, on the other hand, is a term that moves the discourse towards the point of enunciation, that is, it sets up an action, a time and a place that coincide with those of the person speaking such as 'I', 'here' and 'now'. For instance, 'I have been living here for three years'.

See also *embrayage* and *débrayage*.

Signifier and signified

According to Saussure, words are not symbols corresponding to referents but signs made up of two components: a mark or signifier and a concept or signified. Things themselves, therefore, play no part in the language system. The significance of words is based solely on a system of relationships.

Signifier and signified represent the two fundamental levels of language. The term signifier refers principally to the concrete world of sound and vision. The term signified, on the other hand, relates to the concept or idea expressed by the sound or icon. The relationship of the signifier to the signified has been described by Saussure as that between the front and back of a piece of paper. In other words, the two levels of language are in a relationship of reciprocal presupposition; form and content cannot be disassociated. The word (linguistic sign) 'tree', to give an example, is made up of a sound or written mark (signifier) and also of the idea or concept of a tree (signified).

See also *expression and content.*

Simulacrum

The term simulacrum designates a semblance, an image of something which it is not. According to semiotic theory, the production of models or simulacra is the means by which we make sense of the world.

Semiotics itself uses the concept simulacrum when analysing reality effects and attempting to visualize, or visually represent, structures of meaning, or systems of interpretation. An example would be the canonical narrative schema describing human interaction.

Singular

A singular event is an event that occurs once and is narrated once. An example would be the death of Cathy in *Wuthering Heights.*

A singular event can be compared to a repeated and an iterative event.

See also *iterative* and *repeated event.*

Sociolect

The term sociolect designates a kind of sub-language that characterizes a particular group or class of society and that contrasts one group with another. Cockney English is a sociolect, as is argot in French.

Sociolect can be compared with the term idiolect. The study of sociolects stems from the discipline of socio-semiotics.

See also *idiolect*.

Somatic doing

Used to describe a figurative actor (character), the term somatic refers to two types of physical activity:

(a) to bodily movements such as running or stealing, accomplished by an actor and directed towards a goal. These movements constitute events in the narrative.

(b) to physical gestures or attitudes or miming, that is, bodily activities that signify in themselves (convey a message), that are communicative. For instance, shaking your head to signify 'no'. A distinction can therefore be made between verbal communication and somatic communication.

Spatial programming

Spatial programming refers to the relationship established in a narrative between particular places and stages in the quest of an actor. For Robinson Crusoe in Daniel Defoe's novel of that title, the decisive test is associated with the island. Parallels may thus be established between places and types of action: Robinson's home may be connected with departure and return, and the island with struggle and confrontation.

See also *canonical narrative schema*.

Spatialization

The term spatialization designates the process whereby places and locations are established in a discourse. Like actorialization and temporalization it is a necessary ingredient for a referential illusion or reality effect to work. In line with the temporal organization of discourse, spatial structuring serves the installation of narrative programmes and their sequence. Stages of Little Red Riding Hood's mission are thus linked to (1) her mother's house; (2) the wood; (3) her grandmother's house.

See also *actorialization* and *temporalization*.

Strategy

The term strategy defines any long-term plan designed to achieve a specific goal. A general follows a strategy when trying to defeat the enemy. The government develops a strategy to cope with economic difficulties.

According to semiotic theory, the notion of strategy presupposes a situation of confrontation. It is thus defined in terms of interaction between adversaries both attempting to manipulate the enemy in order to thwart his/her aims and achieve one's own goal. In this sense, *strategy* is contrasted with *tactics*, which relates to the technique of manoeuvring. To give an example: in a chess game, the act of devising a plan which plays on the opponent's presumed responses amounts to strategy. The actual playing, or moving the pieces and using the rules to one's advantage, involves tactics.

See also *tactics*.

Structuralism (French)

The term structuralism designates a range of research activities inspired by linguists and carried out in France in the 1960s in a variety of branches of knowledge. As an intellectual movement it takes as its premise that the sign is made up of two parts (signified and signifier) and that there can be no meaning without difference (Saussure). In other words, elements do not signify in isolation: they only acquire meaning by virtue of their contrast with other elements within a structure. The structuralist method, therefore, is characterized by a search for immanent (underlying) structures and/or the construction of models. It is from the structuralist method that semiotics has developed.

Because of its initial success, structuralist theory very quickly became a kind of fashionable philosophy. As a result, it has frequently been accused of being totalitarian, static or reductionist. In the late 1960s, a counter-movement originated, post-structuralism, which, based on the discovery of the essentially unstable nature of signification, altered and refined the original theory.

See also *semiotics* and *signifier and signified.*

Structure

The Swiss psychologist Jean Piaget defines structure as an arrangement of entities that embodies the following fundamental ideas: (1) *wholeness*, which means it is internally coherent; (2) *transformation*, which means that it is not a static form but one capable of transformational procedures, or that it is not only structured but also structuring; (3) *self-regulation*, which means that in order to validate its laws, it does not have to appeal beyond itself.

This definition of structure has been used extensively by the structuralist movement.

Subject

In semiotic metalanguage, the subject (without any qualifying adjective) normally denotes a narrative function (actant) in the actantial structure of an utterance. In this context, the subject is defined on the one hand by and opposite the object of value that is being pursued; on the other, it exists in relation to the sender (source of values and mandator of the quest).

In a narrative, the position of an actant/subject may be held by any actor (character) who performs an action. The abbreviation, a capital S, is frequently used to designate this role. In *Robinson Crusoe*, Robinson Crusoe is the principal subject. In an article about the economic situation of the country, the government, pursuing the goal of beating the recession, is the main subject.

The concepts of discursive and epistemological subjects refer to different levels of an utterance: the discursive level and the deep level respectively.

See also *discursive subject, epistemological subject* and *narrative subject.*

Subject of doing

The expression subject of doing designates a subject who, in its relationship with an object, brings about a transformation. In the sentence 'Father bought a new car', 'Father' is the subject of doing because he has transformed his position of being without a new car into one of being in possession of a new car.

The subject of doing is also frequently referred to as 'agent' or 'operating agent'. It contrasts with the 'subject of state' or 'patient'.

See also *agent, patient* and *subject of state.*

Subject of state

The expression subject of state designates a subject whose relationship with an object remains unchanged. This kind of relationship is frequently shown in verbs of being or possessing. In the sentence 'My father owns several properties', 'my father' is the subject of state, illustrated by his possessions. Equally, in the sentence, 'Nordic women are blue-eyed and have blond hair', 'Nordic women' is the subject of state.

The term subject of state is also referred to as 'patient' in a narrative programme. It contrasts with the 'subject of doing' (or operating agent) whose performance causes a transformation of state.

See also *agent, patient* and *subject of doing.*

Substance

In the vocabulary of Hjelmslev, the term substance denotes the semantic charge assumed by a semiotic form in order to produce meaning. Meaning, moreover, signifies only in the joint manifestation of two distinct forms which correspond to the two planes (or levels) of language: the level of content, composed of a *form* and a *substance*, and the level of expression, also made up of a *form* and a *substance*.

In speech, for example, the sound we make represents the substance while the separate words we pronounce are based on the linguistic system giving form to the sound. Together, substance (sound) and form (linguistic system) amount to our speech on the level of its expression. Equally, the content of our speech is composed of general ideas or semantic raw material – its substance – which is organized in accordance with rules of grammar, that is, its form.

See also *form* and *expression and content.*

Symbol

In traditional literary usage, a symbol relates a word or idea to a concrete object, scene or action with which – though essentially different – it entertains some kind of semantic connection. Thus, in a particular culture, a rose may be a symbol of love, a bird of freedom, a forest of madness, or water of life. A symbol, therefore, is based on a relationship between two individual units – one figurative, one thematic – whereas a semi-symbol is the product of the relationship between two categories.

In Peirce's semiotics, the term symbol denotes a sign (signifier) whose relationship to its object (signified) is entirely arbitrary or based on convention. An example would be the word 'car' where there is no causal physical link or resemblance between the sign (the word car) and its object. In his system of classification, Peirce distinguishes signs used as symbols from those used as icons or as indices (index).

See also *icon, index* and *semi-symbolic.*

Synchrony

The term synchrony denotes simultaneity of action or events. We talk of synchronous occurrences when events coincide in point of time. For instance, the event of President Kennedy being shot took place at the same time as that of onlookers observing the assassination. The two events therefore occurred in synchrony. Equally, a French film with English subtitles requires synchronization of the two languages in order to be fully understood by a monolingual English audience.

Synchrony is opposed to *diachrony* which refers to events arranged in temporal sequence. Saussure used the couple synchrony/diachrony for the description of language in a contemporary and a historical perspective. In particular, he applied synchrony as a working concept with regard to a coherent language system (*langue*). Since any notion of time, however, presents difficulties when applied to abstract systems, present-day linguistics operates within an atemporal or *achronic* framework.

See also *achrony, diachrony* and *language.*

Synonym

A synonym is a word that has the same meaning as, or is very close in meaning to, another word. Examples: 'She tried to run up the <u>slope</u> but the <u>incline</u> was very steep'; 'He <u>rushed</u> to the bus stop although there was no need to <u>hurry</u>'. In both sentences the underlined words are synonyms.

Synonyms are frequently used to strengthen lexical cohesion within a text.

See also *antonym, coherence* and *cohesion.*

Syntagm

The term syntagm designates two or more lexical units linked consecutively to produce meaning. The combination of an adjective and a noun – such as 'human life' or 'beautiful day' – offers an example of a syntagm. The same applies to the joining of two nouns – as in 'desert wind' – or the sequence of words forming a whole sentence: 'we shall go out'.

See also *paradigm.*

Syntax

The term syntax designates the grammatical arrangement of words and syntagms in a clause or sentence. Traditionally, the term refers to one of the two constituent parts of grammar, the other being morphology, that is, the study of the forms of words. The description of the relationship between words or groups of words, on the other hand, and the establishment of rules governing their organization in a sentence, belong to syntax. Grammatical concepts like 'subject', 'object', 'predicate' or 'attribute' are thus part of the descriptive vocabulary of syntax, just as is the classification of subordinate clauses.

Semiotic theory has adopted the term syntax to define one of the two main components of semiotic grammar, with semantics forming the other. Syntax, here, is relevant to the three levels of meaning. Firstly, there is *elementary syntax*, which together with abstract or conceptual semantics accounts for the production, functioning and understanding of meaning at its deepest level. Camus's novel *L'Etranger*, for instance, deals on the deep level with the themes of 'life' and 'death'. Their relationship and dynamics within the text, however, are illustrated by deep-level syntax, which can be presented visually on a semiotic square.

Secondly, there is the level of story grammar or surface *narrative syntax*, which, according to semiotic theory, underpins all discourse, be it literary, scientific, sociological, artistic, etc. Semiotics, here, makes use of two fundamental narrative models, the actantial narrative schema and the canonical narrative schema, to describe basic structures articulating the quest. In the fairy-tale *Jack and the Beanstalk*, the narrative syntax exhibits positions and stages of action: the actant/subject (Jack), the actant/object of the quest (money and marriage), the actant/opponent (the mayor), etc., or different stages of the quest, for example, that of competence (getting and sowing the bean), or that of performance (climbing the beanstalk and defeating the giant), etc.

Thirdly, there is *discursive syntax*. Here we are concerned with the syntactical arrangement of discursive elements on the textual surface. Narrative structures are put into words, given figurative and linguistic shape and placed in sequence. The actant/subject of *Jack and the Beanstalk* becomes 'Jack' and adopts the thematic roles of 'son' and 'lover'. His actions are arranged in chronological order and placed in a particular space, for instance, at the bottom of the beanstalk or at its top.

See also *actantial narrative schema, canonical narrative schema, discursivization, semantics* and *semiotic square*.

System

Along the lines of the Saussurian division of language into *langue* and *parole*, Hjelmslev separates the general practice of giving meaning to objects into a system (*langue*) and a **process** (*parole*). System here represents the paradigmatic axis of language from which signs are chosen, while process refers to the syntagmatic axis combining the language signs into speech.

Generally speaking, the term system denotes a coherent whole of interdependent elements. Saussure refined this definition by discovering that the system in language resides not so much in its elements but in the relationships they entertain with each other. According to him, a paradigm is made up of associative semantic fields which are differentiated by way of opposition to other fields in the same structure. On the other hand, the relationship of similarity between parts of one paradigm also functions to distinguish that particular paradigm from other paradigms, which thus signify by opposition.

See also *language* and *process*.

T

Tactics

The term tactics designates the science or art of deploying forces or performing manoeuvres in situations of confrontation. Thus a general employs tactics in war; or a person might vote tactically, not to support a party but to prevent the election of another party.

Semiotic theory contrasts the notion of *tactics* with that of *strategy*. While tactics refers to a purposeful procedure or the means to achieve an end, strategy relates to the stage of planning and manipulation. Political strategy, for instance, aims to seduce the electorate with promises. Fixing the date of a general election, on the other hand, is the result of tactical manoeuvring.

See also *strategy*.

Temporalization

The term temporalization denotes the process whereby the temporal dimension is installed in a discourse. Like spatialization and actorialization, it is a necessary ingredient for a referential illusion or reality effect to work. Moreover, the element of time needs to be present to turn a narrative arrangement into a story. If Cinderella's going to the ball did not *precede* the search for the owner of the lost slipper and if her happiness *after* the prince has found her was not opposed to her *earlier* unhappiness, there would be no meaning to the story and no tale.

See also *actorialization* and *spatialization*.

Terminative

A terminative term is an aspectual term describing the end of a process. It indicates that a transformation is completed and is frequently conveyed through the use of the simple past (the past historic and perfect tense in French), or the narrative present: 'He left the room'; 'He leaves the room'.

The beginning of a process, on the other hand, is indicated by the use of an inchoative term.

See also *durative* and *inchoative*.

The word text is used in linguistics to refer to any passage, spoken or written, that as a result of the processes of cohesion and coherence forms a unified whole.

See also *coherence* and *cohesion*.

Thematic role

An actor possesses a thematic role if s/he is described in terms of 'themes' such as those of doctor, teacher, carpenter, housewife. These 'themes' are socially defined, stereotyped functions. A character in a story building a house has the thematic role of builder.

The expression thematic role relates to the figurative level of a text and should therefore not be confused with that of actantial role, which is more abstract and relates to the function of a narrative position.

See also *actant* and *actor*.

Thematization

The term thematization refers to the process whereby an enunciator or enunciatee invests figurative discourse with abstract themes. When reading a story mentioning 'clothes', for example, the expression remains ambiguous until it is thematized, in other words, until the enunciator tells us whether to interpret these clothes as a sign of 'wealth' or 'poverty'. A narrative about a poor man getting married and finding employment might be said to establish the themes of success and happiness finding their figurative expression in money earned and a beautiful house.

See also *theme and rheme*.

Theme and rheme

Used widely in discourse analysis, these terms concern the arrangement of information in a sentence or utterance and the importance that the speaker/writer wishes to accord to a particular item.

Theme is a formal grammatical category which refers to the initial element in a clause serving as the point of departure for the message. It is the element around which the sentence is organized and to which the writer/speaker wishes to give prominence. Everything that follows the theme, i.e. the remainder of the message or part in which the theme is developed, is known as the *rheme*. A message, therefore, consists of a theme combined with a rheme. Compare the following sentences:

> (A) The boys mugged the old woman. (B) The old woman was mugged by the boys.

In the first sentence the theme is 'the boys': it is the boys and what the boys did that is of primary interest. Information about who was mugged is secondary, i.e. the rheme. In the second sentence, on the other hand, it is the fate of the victim, the old woman and what happened to her, that is of primary interest (theme).

In semiotic theory, theme is opposed to **figure**. In other words, where figurative elements in discourse are essential ingredients in the construction of a reality effect, themes relate to concepts, to the signified that cannot be perceived by the senses. Thus themes such as 'love', 'hate' and 'evil' are not perceptible in themselves, while their expression in gestures of 'love' or 'hate', for instance, is figurativized and perceived by the senses.

See also *thematization*.

Thymic

Situated on the deep level of an utterance, the thymic category relates to the world of feeling and of emotions. It spans the notion made up by the two poles euphoria versus dysphoria and forms the basis of positive/negative evaluation. In other words, it gives rise to an axiological system – a characteristic of all discourse. To give an example: believing a statement to be true involves not only weighing what is being said for its accuracy but also evaluating it positively.

In recent years attention has been focused on the thymic dimension of narrative. This relates to the feelings of euphoria or dysphoria (i.e. pleasant or unpleasant) experienced by the actors. In other words, the thymic dimension, on the narrative level, is concerned with states of mind (*états d'âme*) or feelings rather than with actions (which belong to the pragmatic dimension) or knowledge concerning these actions (which belongs to the cognitive dimension).

When undertaking semiotic analysis, these states of mind or feelings can be correlated with the stages of a narrative programme. They can, for example, describe a state of disjunction or of conjunction with the object of value. In the fairy-tale *Cinderella*, the young girl's lack of means and of family sympathy is expressed in her disjunction from these objects of value as well as in her feeling of unhappiness that accompanies the disjunction. Equally, Cinderella's conjunction with the prince, her love, at the end of the tale also shows the transformation of her unhappiness into joy being accomplished.

See also *cognitive* and *pragmatic*.

Topic space

The term topic space designates the place where the narrative transformation takes place, i.e. where the principal subject undergoes a change of state. In *Treasure Island* the sea voyage and the island can be considered topic spaces.

Topic space itself can be divided into two categories:

(1) *paratopic space*: this is the space where the qualifying test takes place. The sea journey in *Treasure Island*, or the beanstalk in *Jack and the Beanstalk*, can be considered paratopic spaces.

(2) *utopic space*: this is the space of the principal action where the object of the quest is at stake. The island represents the utopic space in *Treasure Island*, as does the giant's house in *Jack and the Beanstalk*. In Cinderella's quest to go to the ball, the ballroom constitutes an utopic space.

See also *heterotopic space* and *utopic space*.

Toponym

A toponym is a designation of space by a proper noun. The words 'Paris', 'Jupiter', 'Mount of Olives' or 'the Mediterranean Sea', for example, are toponyms. Together with the names of people and time notations, toponyms contribute to the construction of a referential illusion (illusion of the real). They are associated, therefore, with the figurative level of meaning.

See also *anthroponym* and *chrononym*.

Traitor

The traitor or false hero designates one of Propp's seven spheres of action. These were later reduced by Greimas to three pairs of opposed actants (the actantial schema). The semiotic terms 'opponent' and 'anti-subject' subsume the Proppian categories of villain and traitor (false hero).

See also *actantial narrative schema, Propp* and *villain.*

Transformation

A transformation is the passage from one state of affairs (State 1) to another, its opposite (State 2).

State 1 ——————— T ———————➤ State 2

The theft of John's money from his house can be expressed thus:

Presence of money	Theft	Absence of money
State 1 ———————	T ———————➤	State 2

The transformation can correspond to the performance of the subject, who thereby becomes a subject of doing. In order for there to be any story (a narrative) there must be a transformation.

Truth

In general terms, the word truth designates conformity with fact, agreement with reality. In semiotic theory, the notion of truth is replaced with that of *truth-telling* or veridiction. The process of truth-telling here is connected with the circulation of knowledge and the modes of being (*être*) and seeming (*paraître*). Thus any utterance exhibits signs which allow for it being read as true, false, pretending or a downright lie. Whether or not we believe a political statement to be true, for example, depends on our knowledge of the subject-matter and/or on whether the politician seems truthful to us.

Within the context of truth-telling, the semiotic square of veridiction establishes truth as the metaterm generated by the opposing terms being (*être*) and seeming (*paraître*), both of which illustrate different sides of the concept of truth.

See also *metaterm* and *veridiction.*

Uncertainty

Within the epistemic modal category, uncertainty is the contradictory term for certainty. It designates the modal position 'not-believing-to-be', and can be mapped onto a semiotic square as follows:

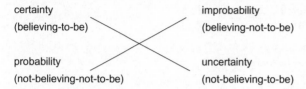

certainty   improbability
(believing-to-be)   (believing-not-to-be)

probability   uncertainty
(not-believing-not-to-be)   (not-believing-to-be)

Example: Mother is <u>certain</u> her child is at school = she believes him to be there and does not believe him not to be there. However, the child is <u>not certain</u> his mother is at home = it is <u>probable</u> that she has gone out shopping.

The different (or changing) positions of certainty and uncertainty of the two actors (mother and child) can be plotted on the above square.

See also *epistemic modalities* and *semiotic square.*

Utopic space

The term utopic space designates the space in which the decisive test takes place and where performances are realized. Utopic space is contrasted with paratopic space. In Zola's *Germinal*, the mine Le Voreux where the miners fight their principal battle for survival constitutes the utopic space. In *Cinderella*, the ballroom where Cinderella encounters the prince constitutes the utopic space.

See also *topic space.*

Utterance

The term utterance designates any entity that is endowed with meaning. It is usually employed with the broad meaning of statement, both oral and written.

Utterance   According to semiotic theory, an utterance can be made by any actant able to produce meaning. Thus a spatial utterance would be a statement made about space, objects, their relationship and transformation: e.g. 'The road meanders through the village', or 'The sun burns down from a lead blue sky. The earth is thirsty'. A visual utterance may signify through shape and colours.

Value

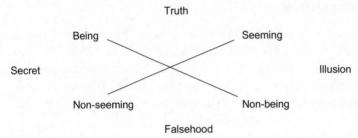

See *object of value.*

Veridiction

The term veridiction designates the process of truth-telling in a story. This is connected to the circulation of knowledge, or lack of it, within a text: some actors know more than others about what is happening in the narrative; some are being deceived, others misunderstand, etc. The reader (enunciatee) may also be enlightened or kept in the dark. In Agatha Christie's novels the enunciator witholds vital information from the enunciatee (reader) until the very end. The modal categories of truth, falsehood, of secret and of illusion thus come into play. The following **semiotic square** of veridiction emerges. It is based on the changing modes of being (*être*) and seeming (*paraître*):

Truth

Being   Seeming

Secret   Illusion

Non-seeming   Non-being

Falsehood

This square allows us to situate modal positions and plot potential trajectories of knowledge. Thus, for example, the detective in a murder story investigates a suspect who <u>seems</u> to have committed the deed but who <u>is not</u> guilty. The true murderer, on the other hand, may at first <u>not</u> <u>seem</u> to be the killer he actually <u>is</u> but is eventually revealed to combine both <u>being</u> and <u>seeming to be</u> a murderer.

See also *modalities* and *semiotic square.*

Villain

In Propp's terminology, the villain belongs to one of the seven spheres of action of the folk-tale. Its principal function is the fight or struggle with the hero. In semiotics, the term villain has been replaced with those of **opponent** and **anti-subject**. Both opponent and anti-subject are part of the three pairs of opposed actants to which Greimas has reduced and regularized Propp's seven spheres of action of the folk-tale.

Most stories present two narrative trajectories, that of the hero (the subject) and that of the villain (the anti-subject); they are only differentiated by their euphoric or dysphoric moralizing connotation. In the film *Batman*, Batman is the hero and the Joker plays the part of the anti-hero. In *Star Wars*, Luke Skywalker's quest is to save the universe from the Emperor and from Darth Vader whose goal it is to take it over. Subject and anti-subject here have their own narrative programmes. We speak of opponent when a villain's main function is to hinder or obstruct the subject's quest without having a conflicting quest of its own. A locked door is an opponent if you are trying to get out. A storm can be an opponent if you want to reach a port.

See also *actantial narrative schema*.

Virtualization

The term virtualization refers to one of the two basic modes of semiotic existence: virtual or actual. Virtual here denotes that which is in a state of simple possibility, but which in its essence contains the main conditions for its realization, in other words, it means possible/ potential. Accordingly, virtualizing modalities are wishing (*vouloir*) and having to do or to be (*devoir*).

Taking language as an example, virtual existence characterizes the paradigmatic axis and actual existence the syntagmatic axis. To put it another way: virtual existence is represented by the language system (*langue*) as opposed to its actualization in the process of speaking (*parole*). The category virtual/actual thus characterizes the relationship between system and process.

With regard to the semiotic model of the narrative, the couple virtualization/actualization has been replaced by the ternary virtualization/actualization/realization in order to describe accurately all possible modes of junction between a subject and an object. Thus before any junction has taken place, subjects and objects are said to occupy *virtual* positions; they are *actualized* when the two actants are disjoined; and they are *realized* once subject and object are conjoined. A person and a car are in virtual positions while the person is only wishing to possess it. We speak of realization once the car has been acquired and of mere actualization if the money has been saved but the car not yet purchased, or if – for non-payment for example – it has been reclaimed by its vendor.

See also *actualization* and *realization*.

Z

Zoomorphic

The term zoomorphic refers to the attribution of the form or nature of an animal to something, especially a god or superhuman being. In general terms, zoomorphic defines something as having the form of an animal. Characters in fairy-tales taking the form of animals are an example of zoomorphism.

A Semiotic Analysis
of
Sleeping Beauty

Sleeping Beauty*

There once lived a King and Queen who were very unhappy because they had no children. They had been married a long time and had almost given up hope when, to the Queen's great joy, she found she was going to have a baby.

Not long after the baby, a beautiful daughter, was born, the King and Queen arranged a huge Christening party. All the fairies in the kingdom were invited, for the King and Queen knew that they would each give a wonderful gift to the new princess. All that is, except one, whom nobody liked because she was so bad-tempered.

After a magnificent feast, the fairies began to offer their gifts. The first fairy gave the gift of Beauty, the second gave Happiness, the others gave Goodness, Health, Gracefulness and Kindness. The seventh fairy was just stepping forward when the door burst open. In rushed the bad-tempered fairy, furious that she had not been invited to the Christening. Everyone shrank back as she rushed up to the cradle.

'On your sixteenth birthday you will prick your finger with a spindle and die', she hissed spitefully at the baby princess, before disappearing in a puff of smoke. Everyone shivered with horror, but at that moment the seventh fairy, who was also the youngest, stepped forward.

'Take heart', she said to the King and Queen. 'Your daughter will not die. My magic isn't strong enough to break the wicked spell but I can weaken the evil. Instead of dying, the princess will fall asleep for a hundred years.'

The King, hoping to save his daughter, immediately ordered every spinning wheel and spindle in the land to be burned.

For fifteen years, everything went well. The princess grew into the most beautiful, the kindest, the most graceful child anyone had ever seen.

At last, the day of her sixteenth birthday arrived. The King and Queen held a magnificent party for her in their castle. They thought

* Taken from Tim and Jenny Wood, *Favourite Fairy Tales* (London: Conran Octopus, 1988), pp. 4-7.

that this would stop her from finding a spindle on that day and so protect her from the wicked fairy's curse. After the feast, the princess asked if they could all play hide-and-seek.

When it was her turn to hide, the princess ran to the far corner of the castle and found a small doorway she had never seen before. She climbed a spiral staircase to a high tower thinking that this would be a wonderful place to hide. When she reached the top, she found a little room. Inside was an old woman sitting at a spinning wheel.

'What are you doing?' asked the princess, fascinated by the twirling wheel and the whirling spindle, for, of course, she had never seen anything like it.

'I am spinning', replied the old lady cunningly, for she was the wicked fairy in disguise. 'Would you like to try?'

The princess sat down and took the spindle. No sooner had she picked it up than the point of the spindle pricked her finger. At once she fell to the ground as if she were dead. The wicked fairy's curse had come true.

But the good fairy's spell came true, too, for the princess was not dead, only sleeping. Immediately everyone else in the castle fell asleep as well. The King and Queen nodded off on their thrones. The guests dozed off as they looked for the princess. The cook started snoring in front of her oven. All over the castle, nothing could be heard but the gentle sounds of hundreds of people sleeping.

As the years passed by, a great hedge of thorns grew up around the castle. Nearly everyone forgot about the King and Queen and their beautiful daughter.

But one day, a hundred years later, a young prince rode by and saw the great hedge of thorns. He stopped and asked an old man what was behind it. The old man told the prince about the castle. The prince was excited by the story and, impatient to find out whether it was true, he drew his sword and started to hack at the briars.

To his surprise, the thorns seemed to part in front of him and in a very short time he had reached the castle. He went through the open door and was amazed to see all the people inside fast asleep. Every single thing was covered in dust and there were huge cobwebs hanging from the ceiling. He explored all the rooms in turn and finally climbed a spiral staircase to the top of a high tower. There, in a small room, lying on the floor, was the most beautiful girl he had ever seen. She was so lovely that, without thinking, he leaned forward and kissed her.

Immediately his lips touched hers, the spell was broken and the princess opened her eyes. The first thing she saw was the handsome prince. As the prince and princess gazed at each other, they fell in love on the spot.

The prince led the princess gently down the spiral staircase. All around them they could hear the sound of the castle coming to life. The prince asked the King and Queen for permission to marry their beautiful daughter. They agreed, and soon plans were being made for the wedding.

The seven good fairies were invited to the wedding feast. They wished the princess and her prince a long and happy life together.

As for the wicked fairy, nobody knew what happened to her, but she was never heard of again!

A semiotic analysis of the fairy-tale
Sleeping Beauty

The semiotic method presented below has been used for several years now in the teaching of literature to university and other students. The approach has yielded outstanding results, proving itself to be particularly effective in the uncovering of the multiplicity of meanings within – and beyond – the text. When applied to opening paragraphs, the method has also provided a means of access to difficult and challenging works (Calvino, Sartre, etc.). The intention of the present authors, however, is not to be prescriptive: semiotic analysis is open-ended and flexible and can be adopted to meet specific requirements. For instance, a student may wish to concentrate on a particular aspect of a novel such as the treatment of place or of time. In this case the analysis – especially of the discursive level – will restrict itself to these components and it will not be necessary to list all the figurative isotopies. Similarly, depending on the nature of the text, a student may wish to concentrate more time and energy on one level of meaning (see below) than another. S/he may even feel it necessary to omit a particular methodological device (e.g. the semiotic square) if its application to the text yields little of interest or relevance.

Our semiotic analysis of *Sleeping Beauty*, then, will start with a reminder that, in contrast to more traditional literary approaches, semiotics postulates the existence of different levels of meaning. Any analysis of a story will begin, therefore, with what is known as the discursive level, that is, with an examination of the specific words – grammatical items/structures – that are visible on the surface of the text. It will then proceed through a process of decoding to uncover ever deeper and more abstract layers of meaning until we arrive at what Greimas terms the elementary structure of meaning. For precise details on the models used in the analysis of the different textual levels, please turn to the Introduction (pp. 7-13). We will now begin with an examination of the discursive level and focus in the first place on the figurative component of the text.

The discursive level

The figurative component

Figurative elements are those elements in a text that correspond to the concrete physical world and that can be apprehended by the five senses. They are essential ingredients in the construction of a reality effect or illusion of a real world. In other words, their primary function is to create an impression of time, of place and of character.

Let us begin by exploring the vocabulary of *Sleeping Beauty* and grouping together notations relating to place (including objects), time and actors (characters). These groupings of words with similar meanings (i.e. with at least one meaning in common) are known as lexical fields, or, in more strictly semiotic terms, figurative isotopies. The words 'house', 'shop', 'street', for instance, have the meaning 'city' in common ('city' is the common denominator): we say, therefore, that these lexical items belong to the isotopy of the 'city'.

Figurative isotopies in *Sleeping Beauty* (page numbers)

Place	Objects
kingdom 145	gift 145 (3 ×)
land 145	spindle 145 (2 ×), 146 (4 ×)
cradle 145	spinning wheel 145, 146
castle 145, 146 (6 ×), 147	thrones 146
door/doorway 145, 146 (2 ×)	oven 146
place to hide 146	dust 146
inside 146 (2 ×)	cobwebs 146
top 146 (2 ×)	sword 146
room 146 (3 ×)	every single thing 146
spiral staircase 146 (2 ×), 147	thorns 146 (3 ×)
floor 146	briars 146
ceiling 146	
ground 146	
down 146, 147	
high tower 146 (2 ×)	

149

Time

once   145, 146
a long time   145
at that moment   145
sixteenth birthday   145 (2 ×)
for fifteen years   145
a hundred years   145, 146
immediately   145, 146, 147
on that day   146

after the feast   146
no sooner   146
at once   146
in a very short time   146
finally   146
as the years passed   146
but one day   146

Actors (characters)

King   145 (6 ×), 146 (2 ×),
   147
Queen   145 (7 ×),
   146 (2 ×), 147
children   145
baby   145 (3 ×)
daughter   145 (3 ×), 146,
   147
princess   145 (4 ×),
   146 (6 ×), 147 (4 ×)
the fairies   145 (2 ×)
seven good fairies   147
bad-tempered fairy   145 (2 ×)
wicked fairy   146 (3 ×), 147
seventh fairy   145 (2 ×)

everyone   145 (2 ×), 146 (2 ×)
nobody   145, 147
guests   146
cook   146
hundreds of people   146
prince   146 (3 ×), 147 (5 ×)
old man   146 (2 ×)
all   145 (2 ×), 146 (2 ×)
all the people   146
old woman/lady   146 (2 ×)
girl   146

The following isotopies also contribute to the construction of a reality
effect:

States of being

born   145
will fall asleep   145
only sleeping   146
fell asleep   146
hundreds of people
   sleeping   146

opened her eyes   147
and die   145
as if she were dead   146
fast asleep   146
nodded off   146
snoring   146

<u>Social events/celebrations</u>

Christening   145 (2×)   marry   147
feast   145, 146, 147   wedding   147 (2×)
party   145 (2×)

Looking back at these lists of figurative isotopies, the reader may be struck by the relatively sparse nature of the references to place and to objects. Indeed, in keeping with the timeless nature of fairy-tales, it is left to the reader's imagination to fill in the descriptive details – appearance of actors, etc. – and to locate the action within a more specific cultural and historical setting.

Having extracted and made lists of the principal isotopies, the next stage in our analysis will be to look for oppositions. These oppositions can be found (a) either within the individual isotopies or (b) between one isotopy and another.

Oppositions

Place: within this isotopy the following oppositions can be discerned:

(1)	*high*	versus	*low*
	high tower		castle
	the top		ground
	ceiling		floor
	up		down
(2)	*wild/natural*	versus	*cultivated/artificial*
	briars		castle
	hedge of thorns		door/doorway
	hacked		room/tower
			spiral staircase
(3)	*outside*	versus	*inside*
	outside		inside
	hedge of thorns		castle
			door/doorway

With indications of *time*, there is an opposition between durativeness (a continual process) and punctuality (happening at one particular moment in time):

durativeness	versus	*punctuality*
a long time		on your sixteenth birthday
for fifteen years		the day ... arrived
as the years passed by		at once
		one day ... a hundred
		years later

For *actors*, the key oppositions that emerge are old versus young, fairies versus humans, male versus female:

old	versus	*young*
old woman/lady		baby
old man		daughter
		new princess
		baby princess
		young prince
		girl

fairies	versus	*humans*
all the fairies		King and Queen
seventh fairy		daughter/princess
bad-tempered/		old lady/guests/cook
wicked fairy		prince/old man

male	versus	*female*
king		Queen
prince		daughter/princess
old man		bad-tempered fairy
		old lady

Within this isotopy of the actors there is also an opposition between plural and singular. Notations such as 'all the fairies', 'everyone', 'all the people', 'all the rooms' are contrasted with references to individual people and places.

And finally, within the isotopy of *states of being*, notations of 'death' are contrasted with those of 'life'; notations of 'sleep' with those of 'awake'.

We must now ask ourselves: What do these oppositions signify? With what values are they being invested by the narrator? As Denis Bertrand has commented,[1] the figurative level makes no sense on its own, it only acquires meaning in relationship to a subject – the narrator – and to the feelings and judgements of this narrator. It is at this point in our analysis, therefore, that we bring to bear what is known as the thymic category – the category related to the world of emotions/feelings and situated at the deep level of the utterance. This category is articulated in the opposition euphoria versus dysphoria (pleasant versus unpleasant) and gives rise to a basic positive/ negative evaluation.

In *Sleeping Beauty* the opposition euphoria versus dysphoria is of particular significance in the construction of the actors. As is customary in the fairy-tale, divisions between pleasant and unpleasant, happy and sad, positive and negative are very clear-cut and unambiguous. The reader is left in no doubt as to where her/his sympathies should lie.

Bearing this in mind, we can extract the following isotopies and oppositions:

(1) The isotopy of the emotions with the opposition euphoria versus dyphoria:

euphoria	versus	*dysphoria*
joy		unhappy
happiness		bad-tempered
excited		furious
surprise		spitefully
amazed		hissed
fell in love		with horror
happy life		

Here positive emotions are associated with one group of actors – the King, Queen, Princess, Prince and seven fairies – whereas the negative are linked (with one exception at the beginning) with the wicked fairy. A process of evaluation is clearly taking place, producing a second grouping:

(2) The isotopy of evaluative terms (physical and moral) with the opposition positive versus negative:

	positive	versus	*negative*
physical	beautiful		
	beauty		
	lovely		
	wonderful		

	positive	versus	*negative*
	magnificent		
	graceful		
	gentle		
	handsome		
	health		
moral	goodness		evil
	kindness		wicked
	kindest		curse
	good		cunningly

Positive physical terms are associated with the princess – beauty, grace, health. These are coupled with positive moral terms: goodness, kindness. The prince is described as handsome but he is not invested explicitly with any moral attributes. Implicitly, however, he could be linked to curiosity ('impatient to find out whether it was true', p. 146) and determination. The other actors in the story are devoid of any physical attributes. The fairies, for example, are evoked in exclusively moral terms: the seven good fairies and the one wicked one.

Figurativity and grammatical/syntactical features

The illusion of the real may be strengthened through the use of linguistic devices such as repetition, ellipsis, active/passive, nominalization and cohesive markers. In our particular version of *Sleeping Beauty*, adapted for very young children, the sentence structure is very simple. What is striking is the frequent use of temporal connectors, particularly at the beginning of sentences, for instance: 'there once', 'not long after', 'after a magnificent feast', 'on your sixteenth birthday', 'for fifteen years', 'at last', 'no sooner', 'at once', 'immediately', 'as the years passed by'. The effect is to heighten the drama and pace of a narrative in which the passage of time is itself an important theme.

Another interesting device is the use of repetition – a characteristic feature of writing for children. Nouns are frequently employed to refer to people where it would be more customary to use a pronoun. For instance, the terms 'the wicked fairy' and 'the good fairy' are repeated in close proximity. The effect once more is to heighten the drama by foregrounding the opposition between good and evil. A sense of symmetry is conveyed, of a universe that is highly ordered. The almost incantatory repetition of these two sets of terms in the last paragraph has the effect of reassuring the child that the threat has been lifted, and that the good is restored.

Further linguistic devices worthy of attention include the use of lists (e.g. 'The King and Queen ..., The guests ..., The cook ...', p. 146), the frequent positioning of the subject (human) at the beginning of a sentence and finally, the marked preference for the active voice.

The enunciative component

The enunciative strategies are clearly those of traditional story-telling. The narrator is third-person and extra-diegetic (i.e. not an actor in the story). This hidden narrator is also omniscient in that the reader has access to the thoughts and emotions of all the actors. The story is told in the past, we are kept at a distance from the events recounted; indeed, telling itself becomes a narrative motif: it is the old man's account of what happened in the castle that prompts the prince to embark on his quest.

Looking at the use of modality – the degree of the speaker's adherence to a statement – the utterances are of a categorical nature. They express certainty on the part of the narrator, there are no tentative utterances suggesting probability or possibility. An impression of narratorial distance and of complete objectivity is thereby conveyed.

At the same time, however, the presence of a narrator – of a subjectivity – can be discerned indirectly in the abundant use of evaluative terms. The sharp divisions between positive and negative, good and evil that we analysed above suggest a particular interpretation of reality or vision of the world.

The enunciative strategies employed in *Sleeping Beauty* thus contribute to a strong sense of reality and to a fictive world whose authenticity is never open to doubt or to questioning. The explicit and clearly delineated categorization – whether in terms of space, time or the actors – serves to reassure the reader, and the child in particular, suggesting a world that is stable and inherently meaningful.

The narrative level

The next stage in our analysis will be an examination of what is known as the narrative level. More abstract than the figurative, this is the level of story-structure proper, that is, the level at which operate underlying universal narrative models. (See also Introduction, pp. 9–12.)

These models can be applied globally to a whole story and/or they can be applied to smaller units or episodes. In order to decide on our approach, it may be helpful to answer the following question: What is (are) the principal event(s)? In other words, what is (are) the principal transformation(s)? If we are having difficulty in selecting key transformations, it may be useful to try to summarize the plot in one or two sentences. It may also help to look at the end of the story – the final event – and compare it with the beginning.

In *Sleeping Beauty* two principal transformations are apparent:

(1) the princess pricks her finger and falls to sleep for a hundred years;

(2) after a hundred years a prince arrives, wakes her (breaks the spell) and marries her.

These transformations are also marked on the surface level by actorial and temporal disjunctions: after the feast (her birthday party), the princess meets an apparently new actor (an old woman) who gives her the spindle with which she pricks her finger (p. 146); another new actor (the prince) arrives on the scene 'one day, a hundred years later' (p. 146). The story thus falls neatly into two parts or two major episodes (narrative programmes). Our analysis will therefore mirror this pattern. The divisions will be: Part 1: from the beginning to 'Nearly everyone forgot about the King and Queen and their beautiful daughter' (p. 146); Part 2: from 'But one day, a hundred years later' (p. 146) to the end.

We begin by examining the distribution in each of the two parts of the text of the six/seven key narrative roles outlined in the *actantial narrative schema* (see also Introduction, pp. 9–10):

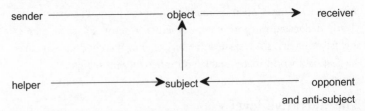

The following questions should be asked of the text:

1. Who (person or persons) is the subject of the quest? The subject is usually the main protagonist but the role can also be enacted by a group of people such as the miners in Zola's *Germinal.*

2. Who or what is the object of the quest? Is there more than one object? The object may be concrete, such as money, or abstract, such as knowledge.

3. Does the subject have helpers and/or opponents? If so, who or what are they?

4. Who is the anti-subject and what is the goal of the anti-subject's quest? An anti-subject, unlike an opponent, possesses its own goal or quest which is in opposition to that of the subject.

5. Who or what is the sender? In other words: what motivates the quest of the subject?

In Part 1 of *Sleeping Beauty* the distribution of narrative roles can be envisaged as follows:

Subject: the subject of the quest is the collective actor, the King and Queen.

Object: the quest has two objects, one concrete (or pragmatic) and one abstract (or cognitive). Concrete: to preserve the life of their daughter and to prevent the wicked fairy's spell from coming true. Abstract: to protect their daughter from all evil and to preserve the gifts/values of Beauty, Happiness, Goodness, Health, Gracefulness and Kindness that she embodies. To see the triumph of good over evil.

Helper: an implied helper are the subjects of the King and Queen who try to burn all the spinning wheels in the land. The magnificent party on the princess's sixteenth birthday is also designed as a helper: 'they thought that this would stop her from finding a spindle on that day' (pp. 145-6).

Opponent: the princess's desire to play hide-and-seek as well as her curiosity concerning the spinning wheel function as opponents.

Sender: the sender of the parents' quest to preserve the life of their daughter is the wicked fairy's curse that the good fairy can only weaken.

Anti-subject: the principal anti-subject is the wicked fairy herself, who, in the guise of an old woman, lures the princess into touching the

157

spinning wheel. The object of her quest is the destruction of the princess's life, that is, her goal is in conflict with that of the King and Queen. Her own sender is her desire for revenge.

The quest of the King and Queen fails: they do not succeed in protecting their daughter from evil. The quest of the wicked fairy succeeds (partially) in that the princess pricks her finger and falls to the ground 'as if she were dead' (p. 146). The quest of the good fairy also succeeds, however, in that the princess sleeps rather than dies. To put more abstractly, the values of Beauty, Happiness, Goodness, Heath, Gracefulness and Kindness lie dormant rather than being destroyed altogether.

Having examined the distribution of narrative roles in Part 1 of *Sleeping Beauty*, we go on to divide the quest into a number of logical stages in accordance with the *canonical narrative schema*. (See also Introduction, pp. 11–12.) These stages are:

The contract

The contract is enacted in two episodes in the text: (1) the wicked fairy's curse and (2) the good fairy's desire to weaken the curse by changing death to sleep. By pronouncing the curse whose effect the good fairy can only mitigate, the wicked fairy incites in the King and Queen the desire and necessity to protect their daughter (both from death and falling to sleep): 'hoping to save his daughter' (p. 145) and implicitly to preserve the gifts she embodies. The King and Queen, now in possession of the modality of wanting-to-do and of having-to-do, become virtual subjects of a global narrative programme or quest.

The qualifying test

Hoping to acquire the ability to carry out his quest (a being-able-to-do), the King orders every spindle in the land to be burnt. However, his efforts meet only with partial success: we learn later that not all the spindles are destroyed. His competence is undermined by an anti-subject, the wicked fairy. Her intention is to harm the princess and, being in possession of supernatural, magic powers, she is stronger than the King.

The decisive test

The arrival and celebration of the princess's sixteenth birthday is the principal event (transformation) towards which the whole story has been moving; it is also the moment of confrontation between two opposing parties or forces. In this confrontation it is the wicked fairy – with her lure – who prevails over the father's attempts to protect his daughter.

The glorifying test

It is at this stage in the quest that the reader learns of the outcome of the decisive test, whether, for example, it has failed or succeeded. In other words, it is at this point that the decisive action is being evaluated. The princess falls asleep: it can be said, therefore, that the parents have failed in their quest to protect their daughter from the effects of evil. The narrator interprets the action of falling asleep as follows: 'At once she fell to the ground as if she were dead. The wicked fairy's curse had come true.' And the next paragraph adds: 'But the good fairy's spell came true, too, for the princess was not dead, only sleeping' (p. 146).

This global narrative programme of the quest in the first part of the story is preceded by a couple of significant episodes (smaller narrative programmes). We recall here that a narrative programme designates a narrative unit expressing a transformation in the relationship between a subject and an object.

At the very beginning of the tale, the King and Queen are introduced as disjoined from their objects of value: a child and happiness. At the end of the paragraph, they are presented as conjoined with these objects: a baby and joy. This is followed by an episode conveying a similar narrative programme. The subject, the seven fairies, give to the princess a number of gifts which she thus acquires through a process of attribution. It is these objects (Beauty, Health, etc.) that, as we have seen, are at stake when the wicked fairy triggers the quest.

Let us now look at the second half of *Sleeping Beauty*, Part 2, commencing with the arrival of the prince (p. 146) and continuing to the end.

In the distribution of narrative roles in this section, the following pattern emerges:

Subject: the prince.

Object(s) of the quest: he wishes to discover if the old man's story about the princess is true. His aim, therefore, is to see the princess and implicitly (by reference to other familiar versions of the tale) to be the one who awakens her with a kiss. The object of his quest, again implicitly, may also be the pursuit of the values of Beauty, Kindness, etc., that is, the values represented by the gifts of the fairies, as well as that of love.

Helper(s):   the prince's own impatience and impetuosity, 'impatient to find out whether it was true' (p. 146), together with his sword, are helpers.

Opponent(s):   the thorns and briars are initially his opponents: he 'started to hack at the briars' (p. 146), only to be transformed into helpers: 'the thorns seemed to part in front of him' (p. 146).

Sender: with his story of the princess, the old man implants in the prince the desire to go on this quest.

Anti-subject: the prince meets with no resistance. A potential anti-subject, the wicked fairy, does not appear on the scene.

Let us now divide the prince's quest into the logical stages of *the canonical narrative schema*:

The contract

The old man arouses in the prince the desire to go on a quest. The prince accepts the contract and decides to act on his desire.

The qualifying test

The prince chops down the briars and thorns. By overcoming this obstacle he acquires the ability (a being-able-to-do) to attain his goal. In other words, he possesses the necessary competence enabling him to reach the castle and the princess.

The decisive test

The arrival in the small room in the high tower of the castle and kissing the princess constitute the decisive test or principal performance.

We learn that the decisive test has been successful: the princess wakes up, the spell is broken, prince and princess fall in love. The marriage, a further episode in the glorifying test, can be considered a reward for the prince and a confirmation of the triumph of good – love and happiness – over evil. The wicked fairy's curse no longer has any power: 'nobody knew what happened to her, but she was never heard of again' (p. 147).

Finally, a global view of the whole story – Part 1 plus Part 2 – still defines the King and Queen as the subject of a quest to protect their daughter from evil and death. In this perspective, however, the prince and his actions function as helper and the overall quest can be deemed successful.

The deep level

After analysing the discursive and narrative levels of meaning, we go on to examine the deep level, known also as the thematic level. This is the level of the abstract or conceptual: it relates to the inner world of the mind as opposed to the outer physical world of the figurative level. Most importantly, it is the level at which are articulated the fundamental values of the text. But how do we arrive at these values?

Let us begin by looking for the fundamental opposition(s) or transformation(s) underlying the text. To facilitate this task, it may be helpful to ask the following questions:

– Can we reduce all the oppositions found on the figurative and narrative levels to one or two basic umbrella oppositions that can function as a common denominator for the text?
– What are the two most abstract poles of meaning between which the text moves?
– What fundamental transformation of values is at stake? Here it might help to bear in might the object of the quest(s).

In *Sleeping Beauty*, a key opposition is that between evil and good. This opposition can be seen as an umbrella term encompassing on the figurative level the passage from high to low, sleep to awake, individual isolation to community.

The fundamental transformation between two poles of abstract meaning can be mapped out on a *semiotic square* (see also Introduction, pp. 12-13). With regard to evil and good, the diagram illustrates relationships of contrariety and of contradiction (evil and non-evil). It also allows for the transformation in the story to be plotted.

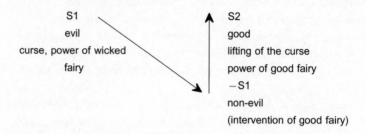

S1
evil
curse, power of wicked
fairy

S2
good
lifting of the curse
power of good fairy
−S1
non-evil
(intervention of good fairy)

This transformation between evil and good parallels that between death and life:

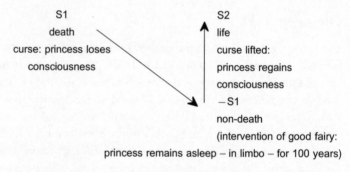

S1
death
curse: princess loses
consciousness

S2
life
curse lifted:
princess regains
consciousness
−S1
non-death
(intervention of good fairy:
princess remains asleep − in limbo − for 100 years)

A third semiotic square could express these transformations in terms of the more specific values represented by the princess:

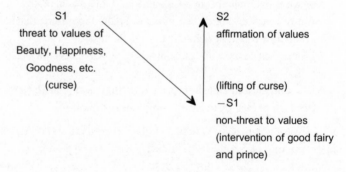

S1
threat to values of
Beauty, Happiness,
Goodness, etc.
(curse)

S2
affirmation of values

(lifting of curse)
−S1
non-threat to values
(intervention of good fairy
and prince)

Text and context

Having ascertained the universal values underlying the text, we then open up the analysis to broader considerations of socio-political and cultural context. What additional values can be brought to bear on the text by the contemporary reader? How relevant is *Sleeping Beauty* to us today? Does the story, like many fairy-tales, lend itself to a multiplicity of levels of interpretation?

We would like to suggest, by way of introduction to this wider canvas of meaning, the following readings which are, of course, by no means exclusive.[2]

A. Sleeping Beauty *can be envisaged as the embodiment of stereotypical attitudes*

As such, the story becomes a vehicle for strengthening social prejudice and social inequality in contemporary society. These attitudes – those generally associated with the traditional fairy-tale and with nineteenth-century romantic fiction – are prevalent in today's media and entertainment literature:

1. Men are active and women are passive. A woman needs the love of a man in order to truly exist, to bring out qualities that lie dormant. It is of course the prince who brings about the key transformation in *Sleeping Beauty*. He also possesses two important actantial roles, that of subject of a quest and of helper. This contrasts with the princess, who appears uniquely in the role of object of someone else's quest (be it that of the parents, the wicked fairy or the prince). In her versions of well-known fairy-tales, Angela Carter challenges this traditional distribution of gender roles: in Bluebeard's *The Bloody Chamber*, for example, it is the mother, arriving on her gallant steed, who finally rescues the heroine from the clutches of her husband.[3]

2. The story attaches great importance to the value of physical beauty – we noted the recurrence of this term in our examination of the figurative component. Implicitly, therefore, it is the beautiful people (the princess and the prince) who are successful in life and who attain their heart's desire. The text thereby legitimizes certain current practices: the tendency, for example, to offer the best jobs to the best-looking. It thus ignores any contemporary concern with the

notion of human/civil rights (rights of the disabled, etc.). As the concept of beauty is itself largely culturally determined, its overvaluation could fuel feelings of racism and xenophobia.

3. The story also links moral worth with physical beauty. As a baby, the princess is given the gifts of Beauty, Goodness and Kindness (in addition to those of Happiness, etc.). The handsome prince is implicitly associated with bravery: he has the courage and temerity to hack down the thorns around the castle. This linking of beauty with moral value is itself, of course, challenged by some conventional fairy-tales such as *Beauty and the Beast* (although the Beast eventually turns back into a handsome prince). It is further subverted by Angela Carter in, for example, her story *The Tiger's Bride*: here Beauty, far from being presented as good, is clearly attracted by acts of violence, sado-masochism and sexual perversion.[4]

4. *Sleeping Beauty* also associates beauty with, on the one hand, youth and, on the other, sexual love. From this point of view, too, the text can be said to reinforce a dominant ideology in Western society: it encourages an overestimation of youth and an accompanying devaluation of the later equally important stages in human life. Such attitudes lead to the dismissal and disparagement of older people in particular. These assumptions are forcefully challenged by, *inter alia*, Gabriel García Márquez in *Love in the Time of Cholera*, where old age sees the blossoming of physical love, beauty and passion.[5]

5. The text can furthermore be said to enact a number of fantasies. Most significant perhaps is the desire for eternal youth, recalling the Faust story. This desire in turn reflects an underlying and all-too-human fear of growing old, of change and of death.

6. In its focus on 'love at first sight', the story finally reinforces a number of stereotyped assumptions concerning the nature of love. The outcome of events – marriage followed by a long and happy life – rests on the supposition that love (together with physical beauty) will endure the test of time.

As a reflection of stereotypical attitudes and fantasies, *Sleeping Beauty* - and similar stories – have an important function within the contemporary debate concerning human/civil rights and how to foster in the younger generation the notion of world citizenship.[6] The story is not a text for passive consumption but demands a critical reading on the part of the reader – be it an adult or a child. As we have seen, this critical reading will necessarily go beyond the confines of the text itself. It should stimulate active discussion encompassing the wider canvas of contemporary social and philosophical issues.

B. *The impact of* Sleeping Beauty *on the reader is not, however, entirely negative*

Indeed, certain aspects of the text call for a positive, more 'liberatory' interpretation, one that is not without its own contemporary relevance. The story presents a self-contained meaningful universe in which the boundaries of good and evil are clearly delineated. In his seminal work *Language and Silence*, George Steiner relates the increasing tendencies in our language usage to blur ethical frontiers to the growth of widespread political inhumanity in the twentieth century (e.g. the Holocaust).[7] In his novel *Le Chercheur d'or* (The Seeker for Gold) the contemporary French writer J. M. G. Le Clézio links the survival of being human, and of meaning itself, to a memory of this vital distinction between good and evil – a memory that is perpetuated in myth and in the fairy-tale.[8]

Not only, however, is the distinction between good and evil clear-cut and unambiguous. As we would also expect from a traditional fairy story, the unfolding of events heralds the triumph of good over evil, the possibility that our goals may be achieved, that our dreams may come true. It thus foregrounds the value of hope – for many the mainspring of all human action – offering a healthy antidote to current tendencies to cynicism. Moreover, this triumph of positive values, be they aesthetic (Beauty), spiritual (Goodness, Kindness) or personal/psychological, takes place against all odds – the power of the wicked fairy is stronger than that of the good one – that is, it takes place against a backdrop of a realistic acceptance of the power of destructive forces within contemporary society. But, however strong these forces, positive qualities and creative energy can never be entirely destroyed. These values remain in a virtual state, in limbo (dormant) waiting to be activated through the initiative of the individual. We may note here the theme of memory in *Sleeping Beauty* and its role in preserving these values from eventual oblivion and death: it is the recounting of the past by the old man that awakens the prince's curiosity to embark on the quest.

In addition to these predominantly moral and socio-political readings of the text, a more strictly mythical/religious interpretation is possible. Our analysis of the figurative component noted the division of space into 'high' and 'low'. This configuration (division) possesses symbolic and, according to Gaston Bachelard, archetypal connotations.[9] The 'high' is linked with semes of myth and magic (the princess pricks her finger and falls asleep). It also represents the spiritual dimension of eternal and universal values – those of Kindness, Goodness, etc. – that cannot be altered or destroyed by time. In contrast, the 'low' is associated with the historic space of social ceremony (christening, marriage, etc.). The princess, herself, inhabits both these dimensions.

Sleeping Beauty presents, therefore, a mythical non-Cartesian view of the world. Like many fairy-tales, it challenges the hegemony of reason, suggesting the workings of powerful unseen and irrational forces. Its insights – meanings – are clearly of relevance to contemporary debates on the nature of the human subject. Indeed, present-day psychologists and philosophers, in their attempt to elaborate ever more complex models of the self, increasingly draw upon folk-tales and myth for their source of inspiration.

Notes

1. Denis Bertrand, 'Narrativity and Discursivity', in *Paris School Semiotics*, vol. 1, trans. and ed. by P. Perron and F. Collins (Amsterdam/Philadelphia: Benjamins, 1989).
2. *Sleeping Beauty* lends itself, for example, to psychological readings. See *inter alia* Bruno Bettelheim, *The Uses of Enchantment: The Power and Importance of Fairy Tales* (London: Thames and Hudson, 1976).
3. Angela Carter, *The Bloody Chamber and Other Stories* (Harmondsworth: Penguin, 1979).
4. *Ibid.*, pp. 51–67.
5. Gabriel García Márquez, *Love in the Time of Cholera*, trans. by Edith Grossman (Harmondsworth: Penguin, 1985).
6. The philosopher Jürgen Habermas, for example, links the concept of world citizenship to an agreed acceptance amongst all nations of a number of key moral values/codes.
7. George Steiner, *Language and Silence* (Harmondsworth: Pelican Books, 1969).

8. J. M. G. Le Clézio, *Le Chercheur d'or* (Paris: Gallimard, 1985).

9. For Bachelard the enclosed space of the attic is also linked to the semes of intimacy and of refuge. See *La Poétique de l'espace* (Paris: Presses Universitaires de France, 1957).

Bibliography

Adam, Jean-Michel, *Le Texte narratif* (Paris: Nathan, 1985).

Ali Bouacha, A. and Bertrand, Denis, *Lectures de récits. Pour une approche sémio-linguistique des textes littéraires; parcours méthodologique de lecture et d'analyse* (Paris: Bureau pour l'Enseignement de la Langue et de la Civilisation Françaises à l'Etranger, 1981).

Arrivé, Michel, 'La sémiotique littéraire', in *Sémiotique. L'Ecole de Paris*, ed. Jean-Claude Coquet (Paris: Hachette, 1982).

Arrivé, Michel and Coquet, Jean-Claude, *Sémiotique en jeu. A partir et autour de l'oeuvre d'A. J. Greimas* (Paris/Amsterdam: Hadès–Benjamins, 1987).

Bachelard, Gaston, *La Poétique de l'espace* (Paris: Presses Universitaires de France, 1957).

Bertrand, Denis, *L'Espace et le sens. Germinal d'Emile Zola* (Paris/Amsterdam: Hadès–Benjamins, 1985).

Bertrand, Denis, 'Le corps émouvant. L'absence. Proposition pour une sémiotique de l'émotion', *La Chouette (Birkbeck College)*, 20 (1988), 46–54.

Bertrand, Denis, 'Narrativity and Discursivity', in *Paris School Semiotics*, vol. 1, P. Perron and F. Collins (trans. and eds) (Amsterdam/Philadelphia: Benjamins, 1989).

Bettelheim, Bruno, *The Uses of Enchantment: The Power and Importance of Fairy Tales* (London: Thames and Hudson, 1976).

Carter, Angela, *The Bloody Chamber and Other Stories* (Harmondsworth: Penguin, 1979).

Cook, Guy, *The Discourse of Advertising* (London: Routledge, 1992).

Costantini, Michel and Darrault-Harris, Ivan (eds), *Sémiotique, phénoménologie, discours: du corps présent au sujet énonçant* (Paris: L'Harmattan, 1999).

Courtés, Joseph, *Introduction à la sémiotique narrative et discursive* (Paris: Hachette, 1976).

Courtés, Joseph, *Sémantique de l'énoncé: applications pratiques* (Paris: Hachette, 1989).

Courtés, Joseph, *Analyse sémiotique du discours: de l'énoncé à l'énoncia-*
tion (Paris: Hachette, 1991).

Courtés, Joseph, *Du lisible au visible* (Brussels: De Boeck, 1995).

Eco, Umberto, *The Role of the Reader: Explorations in the Semiotics of*
Texts (London: Hutchinson, 1981).

Everaert-Desmedt, Nicole, *Sémiotique du récit* (Brussels: De Boeck-
Wesmael, 1989).

Fairclough, Norman, *Critical Discourse Analysis: The Critical Study of*
Language (London: Longman, 1975).

Fairclough, Norman, *Language and Power* (London: Longman, 1989).

Fairclough, Norman, *Discourse and Social Change* (Cambridge: Polity
Press, 1992).

Fairclough, Norman (ed.), *Critical Language Awareness* (London:
Longman, 1992).

Floch, Jean-Marie, *Petites Mythologies de l'oeil et de l'esprit. Pour une*
sémiotique plastique (Paris/Amsterdam: Hadès–Benjamins, 1985).

Floch, Jean-Marie, *Sémiotique, marketing et communication* (Paris:
Presses Universitaires de France, 1990).

Floch, Jean-Marie, *Identités visuelles* (Paris: Presses Universitaires de
France, 1995).

Floch, Jean-Marie, *Une Lecture de Tintin au Tibet* (Paris: Presses
Universitaires de France, 1997).

Fontanille, Jacques, *Le Savoir partagé* (Paris/Amsterdam: Hadès–
Benjamins, 1987).

Fontanille, Jacques, *Les Espaces subjectifs* (Paris: Hachette, 1989).

Fontanille, Jacques, *Sémiotique et littérature: essais de méthode* (Paris:
Presses Universitaires de France, 1999).

Fowler, Roger, *Linguistics and the Novel* (London: Methuen, 1977).

Fowler, Roger, *Linguistic Criticism* (Oxford: Oxford University Press,
1986).

Fowler, Roger, *Language in the News: Discourse and Ideology in the Press*
(London: Routledge, 1991).

Genette, Gérard, *Figures II* (Paris: Seuil, 1969).

Genette, Gérard, *Palimpsestes* (Paris: Seuil, 1982).

Genette, Gérard, *Seuils* (Paris: Seuil, 1987).

Greimas, Algirdas J., *Sémantique structurale* (Paris: Larousse, 1966).

Greimas, Algirdas J., *Du sens: essais sémiotiques* (Paris: Seuil, 1970).

Greimas, Algirdas J., *Maupassant, la sémiotique du texte: exercices*
pratiques (Paris: Seuil, 1976).

Bibliography

Greimas, Algirdas J., *Sémiotique et sciences sociales* (Paris: Seuil, 1976).

Greimas, Algirdas J., *Du sens II: Essais sémiotiques* (Paris: Seuil, 1983).

Greimas, Algirdas J., *De l'imperfection* (Périgueux: Fanlac, 1987).

Greimas, Algirdas J., 'On meaning', *New Literary History*, 20 (1989), 539-50.

Greimas, Algirdas J. and Courtés, Joseph, *Sémiotique, dictionnaire raisonné de la théorie du langage* (2 vols; Paris: Hachette, 1979 and 1986).

Greimas, Algirdas J. and Fontanille, Jacques, *Sémiotique des passions: des états de choses aux états d'âme* (Paris: Seuil, 1991).

Grivel, Charles, *Production de l'interêt romanesque* (The Hague/Paris: Mouton, 1973).

Halliday, Michael and Hasan, Ruqaiya, *Cohesion in English* (London: Longman, 1976).

Hamon, Philippe, *Introduction à l'analyse du descriptif* (Paris: Hachette, 1981).

Hamon, Philippe, 'Un discours contraint', in Gérard Genette and Tzvetan Todorov (eds), *Littérature et réalité* (Paris: Seuil, 1982).

Hawkes, Terence, *Structuralism and Semiotics* (London: Methuen, 1977).

Hénault, Anne, *Les Enjeux de la sémiotique* (Paris: Presses Universitaires de France, 1979).

Hénault, Anne, *Narratologie, sémiotique génerale: les enjeux de la sémiotique 2* (Paris: Presses Universitaires de France, 1983).

Hénault, Anne, *Histoire de la sémiotique* (Paris: Presses Universitaires de France, 1992).

Hodge, Robert and Kress, Günther, *Language as Ideology* (London: Routledge, 1979).

Hodge, Robert and Kress, Günther, *Social Semiotics* (Cambridge: Polity Press, 1988).

'Hommages à A.J. Greimas', *Nouveaux actes sémiotiques*, 25 (1993).

Jakobson, Roman, *Fundamentals of Language* (The Hague/Paris: Mouton, 1975).

Landowski, Eric, *La Société réfléchie: essais de socio-sémiotique* (Paris: Seuil, 1989).

Landowski, Eric, 'Pour une problématique socio-sémiotique de la littérature' in, Louise Milot and Fernand Roy (eds), *La Littérature* (Sainte-Foy: Presses de l'Université de Laval, 1991), pp. 95-119.

Landowski, Eric, 'On ne badine pas avec l'humour: la presse et ses petits dessins', *Humoresques: Sémiotique & Humour*, 4 (Jan. 1993), 43-67.

Landowski, Eric (ed.), *Lire Greimas* (Limoges: Presses Universitaires de Limoges, 1997).

Landowski, Eric, *Présences de l'autre* (Paris: Presses Universitaires de France, 1998).

Le Clézio, J. M. G., *Le Chercheur d'or* (Paris: Gallimard, 1985).

Lévi-Strauss, Claude, *Anthropologie structurale*, I and II (Paris: Plon, 1958 and 1968).

Locke, John, *An Essay Concerning Human Understanding*, ed. Peter H. Nidditch (Oxford: Clarendon Press, 1975/1979).

Márquez, Gabriel García, *Love in the Time of Cholera*, trans. E. Grossman (Harmondsworth: Penguin, 1985).

Martin, Bronwen, *The Search for Gold: Space and Meaning in J. M. G. Le Clézio* (Dublin: Philomel Productions, 1995).

Martin, Bronwen, 'Introduction to semiotic analysis', *La Chouette (Birkbeck College)*, 27 (1996), 7-18.

Martin, Bronwen, *Semiotics and Storytelling* (Dublin: Philomel Productions, 1997).

Martin, Bronwen, 'Spatial figurativity in Marguerite Duras' in C. Rodgers and R. Udris (eds), *Marguerite Duras: lectures plurielles* (Amsterdam: Rodopi, 1998).

Perron, P. and Collins, F. (trans. and eds), *Paris School Semiotics* (2 vols; Amsterdam/Philadelphia: Benjamins, 1989).

Propp, Vladimir, *Morphology of the Folktale*, 2nd edn (Austin: University of Texas Press, 1968); 1st edn (Bloomington: Indiana University Press, 1958).

Ringham, Felizitas, 'Reader-related truth: a semiotics of genre and paratext in early eighteenth century prose fiction in France' (doctoral thesis, University of London, 1994).

Ringham, Felizitas, 'Seduction and commitment in paratext', *La Chouette (Birkbeck College)*, 27 (1996), 29-39.

Ringham, Felizitas, 'Le corps textuel: forme ou substance?', *La Chouette (Birkbeck College)*, 29 (1998), 9-14.

Ringham, Felizitas, 'Riquet à la houppe: conteur, conteuse', *French Studies*, vol. 52, no. 3 (July 1998).

Saussure, Ferdinand de, *Cours de linguistique générale* (first published 1915 from notes of his lectures taken by students).

Bibliography

Scholes, Robert, *Structuralism in Literature: An Introduction* (New Haven/London: Yale University Press, 1974).

Steiner, George, *Language and Silence* (Harmondsworth: Pelican Books, 1969).

Thompson, Stith, *Motif Index of Folk-Literature: A Classification of Narrative Elements in Folk Tales, Ballads, Myths, Fables, Mediaeval Romances, Exemplar Fabliaux, Jest-books, and Local Legends*. 6 volumes (Copenhagen: Rosenkilde and Bagger, 1955-8).

Urbain, Jean-Didier, 'Idéologues et polylogues: pour une sémiotique de l'énonciation', *Nouveaux actes sémiotiques*, 14 (1991), 1-51.

Wilson, W. Daniel, 'Readers in texts', *P.M.L.A.*, 96 (Oct. 1981), 848-63.

Wood, Tim and Jenny, *Favourite Fairy Tales* (London: Conran Octopus, 1988).

Index

A

absence   17
abstract   17
achrony   17
acquisition   18
actant   18
actantial narrative schema
    9-10, 19, 156-8
action   19-20
actor   20
actorialization   20
actualization   21-2
adjudicator   22
aesthetics   22
agent   23
alethic modalities   23
anachronism   23
analysis   24
anaphora   24
anthropomorphic   24
anthroponym   25
antiphrasis   25
anti-sender   25
anti-subject   25
antonym   26
aphoria   26
appropriation   26-7
aspectualization   27
attribution   27
Austin, J. L .   74, 100,
    101
author   28

axiology   28
axiomatic   28

B

Bachelard, Gaston   166
Barthes, Roland   2, 94
being   29
being-able   29-30
believing-to-be   30-1
Benveniste, Emile   66
Bertrand, Denis   119, 152
binarism   31
binary   31

C

canonical narrative schema
    11-12, 32-3
cataphora   33
category   33
certainty   33
chrononym   33
classeme   34
code   34
cognitive   34
coherence   35
cohesion   35-6
collective   36
collocation   36
communication model   36-7
comparative reference   37
competence   38
complementary   39

conative function   39
conceptual   39
concrete   39-40
configuration   40
confrontation   40-1
conjunction   41
conjunction and
    disjunction   41-2
connector   42
connotation   42-3
content   3, 43
context   43-4, 162-6
contract   32, 44-5, 158, 160
contradiction   45
contrary   46
correlation   46
culture   46

D

débrayage/disengagement   47
decisive test   11, 32, 47,
    159, 160
deixis   47-8
demonstrative reference   48-9
denotation   49
descriptive   49
diachrony   50
dialogue   50
diegesis   51
discourse   51
discursive level   6, 8-9, 51-2,
    149-55
discursive subject   52
discursive units   53
discursivization   53
disjunction and conjunction   53
doing/faire   54
donor   54

durative   55
dysphoria   55

E

elementary utterance   56
ellipsis   56
embedding   56
embrayage/engagement   57
emotion   57
enunciative subject   57-8
enunciator/enunciatee   58-9
episteme   59
epistemic modalities   59-60
epistemological subject   60
epistemology   60
euphoria   61
evaluative   61
expression and content   3,
    61-2
expressive function   62

F

Fairclough, Norman   96
figurative   64
figurativization   64
figure   64
focalization   64-5
focalizer   65
form   3, 65
Foucault, Michel   59
function   3, 66

G

generative trajectory   67
Genette, Gérard   51, 94
genre   67
gift   68

glorifying test   12, 33, 68, 159, 161
grammar   69
Greimas, A. J.   2, 4-7, 22, 59, 67, 72, 92, 94, 105, 107, 116, 136, 139-40

H

Halliday, Michael   35, 36, 41, 42, 51, 96, 109, 110
Hasan, Ruqaiya   41, 42
having-to-be   70
having-to-do   70
helper   70
hermeneutics   70
hero   71
heterotopic space   71
hierarchy   71-2
Hjelmslev, Louis   2, 3, 43, 61-2, 65, 66, 79, 83, 84, 104, 116, 127, 130
homologation   72
hypotactic   72

I

icon   73
iconicity   73
identity   73
ideology   73-4
idiolect   74
illocutionary act   74-5
illusion   75
immanence and manifestation   75
inchoative   75
index   76
individual   76

interoceptive/exteroceptive   76
interpretation   76-7
isotopy   9, 77
iterative   77

J

Jakobson, Roman   31, 34, 36-7, 66, 122

K

knowing-how-to-do   78

L

lack   79
language   2-3, 79
language act   80
Lévi-Strauss, Claude   2, 3, 46, 89, 95
lexeme   80
lexia   80
lexical cohesion   81
lexical field   81
lexicology   81
life/death   81-2
listener   82
Locke, John   1

M

manifestation   83
Martinet, A.   66
matter   83
metalanguage   83
metalingual function   83
metaphor   84
metasemiotics   84
metaterm   84-5

metonomy   85
modal   85
modalities   5, 85-7
modalization   87-8
morpheme   88
morphology   88-9
motif   89
myth   89-90

N

narrative pivot point   91
narrative programme   9, 91-2
narrative subject   92
narrative trajectory   92
narrative utterance   92-3
narratology   93-4
narrator/narratee   94
nature   95
negative   95
nominalization   96

O

object of value   97
onomatopoeia   97
opponent   97

P

paradigm   98
paraphrase   98
paratopic   98
passion   98-9
pathematic role   99
patient   99-100
Peirce, C. S.   1, 73, 76, 128
performance   100
performative   100
perlocutionary act   101

personification   101
persuasive doing   101
phatic function   101-2
phoneme   102
phonemics   102
phonetics   102
Piaget, Jean   126
poetic or aesthetic
     function   102-3
polysemy   103
positive   103
Pottier, B.   80
pragmatic   103-4
process   3, 104
Propp, Vladimir   2, 3-4, 5, 54,
     66, 79, 89, 105, 136, 139-40

Q

qualification   103
qualifying test   11, 32, 106-7,
     158, 160
quest   107

R

reader   108
reality   108
realization   108-9
receiver   109
reference   109
referent   109-10
referential cohesion   110
referential function   110
reiteration   111
renunciation   111
repeated event   111
rhetoric   111-12

S

sanction   113
Saussure, Ferdinand de   2-3, 50, 65, 79, 102, 116, 123, 125, 130-1
Searle, John   80
secret   113
seeming   113
semantic category   113-14
semantic field   114
semantics   114-15
seme   115
sememe   115
semic density   115
semiology   2, 116
semiotic square   5-6, 12-13, 116-17, 161
semiotics   1-2, 7-13, 117-18
semiotics of passion   118-20
semi-symbolic   121
sender   121
sender-adjudicator   122
shifter   122
signifier and signified   3, 123
simulacrum   123
singular   123
sociolect   124-5
somatic doing   124
spatial programming   124
spatialization   124-5
Steiner, George   165
strategy   125
structuralism (French)   125
structure   126
subject   126
subject of doing   127
subject of state   127
substance   3, 127-8

symbol   128
synchrony   2, 128
synonym   129
syntagm   129
syntax   129-30
system   3, 130-1

T

tactics   132
temporalization   132
terminative   132
text   133
thematic role   133
thematization   133
theme and rheme   133-4
Thompson, Stith   89
thymic   134-5
Todorov, Tzvetan   94
topic space   135
toponym   135
traitor   136
transformation   136
truth   136

U

uncertainty   137
utopic space   137
utterance   137

V

value   139
veridiction   139
villain   139-40
virtualization   140-1

Z

zoomorphic   142